A School Reader

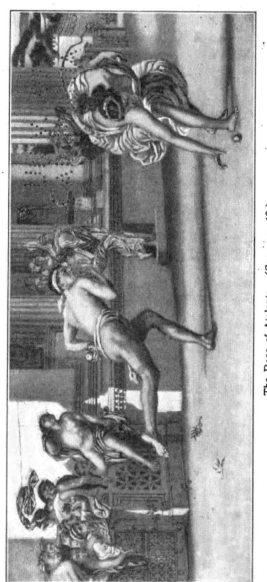

The Race of Atalanta. (See page 10.)

A

SCHOOL READER

THIRD GRADE

BY

FANNY E. COE

TEACHER OF ENGLISH IN THE BOSTON NORMAL SCHOOL
AUTHOR OF "MODERN EUROPE," "OUR
AMERICAN NEIGHBORS," ETC.

NEW YORK ·:· CINCINNATI ·:· CHICAGO
AMERICAN BOOK COMPANY

CLASSIFIED CONTENTS

POETRY

THE PRETERNATURAL

MYTHS

ADVENTURE

HISTORICAL STORIES

(Arranged Chronologically)

HUMOR

ACKNOWLEDGMENTS

THE selections from Lucretia P. Hale, Sarah Orne Jewett, Eliza Orne White, and James T. Fields are used by special permission of Houghton, Mifflin & Co. The extracts from M. P. W. Smith's "Jolly Good Times on a Farm" is used by permission of Little, Brown & Co. The extract from De Segur's "Story of a Donkey" is reprinted by permission of D. C. Heath & Co. "The Land of Story Books" by Stevenson is reprinted by permission of Charles Scribner's Sons. Two extracts from Wyss's "The Swiss Family Robinson" are used by permission of E. P. Dutton & Co., New York.

Thanks are extended to the above-mentioned publishers, and grateful acknowledgment is furthermore rendered to Mr. James Baldwin for the use of two of his "Fifty Famous Stories Re-told" and to Mrs. Emily Huntington Miller for her poem "Little May."

THE LAND OF STORY BOOKS[1]

star'ry   prowled   sol'i tudes

At evening, when the lamp is lit,
Around the fire my parents sit.
They sit at home, and talk and sing,
And do not play at anything.

[1] From "Poems and Ballads," copyright 1895, 1896, by Charles
Scribner's Sons.

TO VIMU[10]

Now, with my little gun, I crawl
All in the dark along the wall,
And follow round the forest track
Away behind the sofa back.

There, in the night, where none can spy,
All in my hunter's camp I lie,
And play at books that I have read
Till it is time to go to bed.

These are the hills, these are the woods,
These are my starry solitudes,
And there the river, by whose brink
The roaring lions come to drink.

I see the others far away,
As if in firelit camp they lay,
And I, like to an Indian scout,
Around their party prowled about.

So, when my nurse comes in for me,
Home I return across the sea,
And go to bed with backward looks
At my dear Land of Story Books.

—ROBERT LOUIS STEVENSON.

THE RACE OF ATALANTA

dam'sel·	quiv'er	Ve'nus
con di'tions	or'a cle	spec ta'tors
At a lan'ta	Hip pom'e nes	li'on ess

Long ago there lived a young princess named Atalanta. She was more like a lad than a maiden. She loved to run, to swim, and to hunt.

A quiver full of arrows hung from her shoulder. In her left hand she carried her bow. Fleet was the deer that could escape her!

Atalanta had had her fortune told. The oracle had said, "Atalanta, do not marry! Harm will come if you do."

The young princess decided to obey the oracle. She had many lovers, but she answered them all in this way: "Let us try a race. If you win, I will be your wife. If you lose, you must die."

These were hard conditions. However, there were some young men ready to try. They asked their friend Hippomenes to be the judge of the race.

"How foolish you are!" cried he. "I would not risk my life for the most beautiful damsel in all Greece."

But when Hippomenes saw Atalanta on the race course, he changed his mind. Her beautiful golden hair floated behind her in a cloud as she ran. Her eyes shone as blue as the sky; her cheeks were pink as the dawn. No one in all the world was so fleet of foot. "She is worth the risk," said Hippomenes.

Atalanta ran far faster than the friends of Hippomenes, and so they all had to die.

While Atalanta was resting, Hippomenes stepped forward. "I will race with you and win," he cried.

"Be warned by the fate of your friends," said the maiden. "I do not wish your death." To herself she added, "I could almost wish him to outrun me."

In the moment before the race, Hippome-

nes prayed to Venus: "Come to my aid, O
Venus. Upon you I depend."

Immediately Venus slipped into his hand
three golden apples. She whispered in his ear
the way to use them.

The signal was given. The young man
and maiden began to race. "Hasten, hasten,
Hippomenes!" cried the spectators. "You
are gaining. One more effort!"

But Hippomenes grew weary; his breath
began to fail him. He threw one of the
golden apples to the ground. Atalanta saw
him and wondered; then she stopped to pick
it up. Hippomenes raced ahead.

The people shouted for joy. But a minute
later Atalanta had passed him. Again he
threw an apple and again he gained on Atalanta.

The goal was very near when Atalanta
passed him the third time.

"Help, Venus!" he cried, and threw down
the last apple far to the right. Atalanta saw
the golden gleam. She hesitated, and then

14

rushed after it. Thus Hippomenes won the race and a beautiful wife.

You would suppose that they would seek Venus at once to thank her for her aid. But Atalanta and Hippomenes were so happy that they forgot every one and everything.

To punish them Venus changed Atalanta to a lioness and Hippomenes to a fierce lion with a tawny mane. Together they draw the car of one of the goddesses. —F. E. Coe.

THE SCHOOL FOR SQUASHES

com mit'tee	ex pres'sion	prod'i gy
dig'ni fied	ob served'	quan'ti ty
doff'ing	op'po site	re spond'ed
ex am i na'tion	par tic'u lar	re tired'

In the afternoon Lois came up, and Millie and she went out to the barn to play. In one of the vacant stables, Mr. Kendall had stored a quantity of crook-necked squashes.

"Let's play keep school with these squashes," said Millie. "The boys aren't around anywhere to bother us, and we can have real fun."

"I slipped out the front door so Roy needn't know I was coming," said Lois.

With an old stump of a broom they swept the stable nicely. Some milking-stools made

good seats for the teacher and the "company," and the squashes were leaned up in a row against the wall opposite.

"Now," said Lois, "we must scratch their names on them with pins, or we never can remember; they look so much alike."

16

" Let's give them the prettiest names we can think of," said Millie.

So, *Louisa, Eva, Helen, Augusta, Rose, Grace, Minnie,* were scratched in big letters on the squashes' smooth skins.

"Let's call this one Mary Jane, she's so homely," said Lois, holding up a dark-colored squash, covered with wart-like bunches.

" No," said Millie, " I don't think we ought to hurt her feelings just because she is homely. She can't help it, you know. Let's call her Florence and play she is really smart."

When every one was named, Millie said, "Now I'll be the teacher, and you'll be the committee to come in to visit the school. Play it's examination day."

Lois retired. Presently, as the class were spelling "Baker" in very loud tones, a rap came at the stable door. Millie went to it.

"Oh! how do you do, Mr. Jones? I am very happy to see you. Won't you walk in?"

Doffing her sunbonnet with an important air, Lois walked in and took a seat on the milk stool. She sat up very stiffly, and looked with a dignified expression at the scholars.

" Now, Grace," said Millie, with a prim air, " let me hear you spell ' candy.' "

" Kan-de," spelt Grace, in a squeaky little voice.

" The next."

" Kan-di."

" No. Florence, spell ' candy.' "

" Can-dy," spelt this prodigy, in loud prompt tones.

" Go to the head."

" That Florence," whispered the teacher to the committee, " is my best scholar."

" She looks as if she might be," politely responded the committee.

" Would you like to hear them do anything in particular ? " asked the teacher.

" Yes, I'd like to hear them say the table of sixes, backward."

" H'm, I'm afraid they don't know it very well. You'd better hear them sing. Class, sing ' One little, two little, three little Indians.' "

As the sweet strains of this song were rising on the air, the school was suddenly interrupted in the most startling manner. Through the scaffolding over the stable a cowhide boot appeared, followed by a long leg, and loud laughing was heard from above.

"The boys have been up there listening all the time!" exclaimed Lois, with a red face.

"It's just as mean as it can be," added Millie, warmly.

Ralph now swung himself down into the manger, followed by Roy and Teddy.

"I wouldn't be a-listening round where I wasn't wanted," observed Millie, loftily.

"We weren't listening. At least we were up there when you came out and then we couldn't help listening, it was such fun. Ralph broke through the scaffolding, or you wouldn't have found us out."

"Well, then, go away and let us alone."

"No, sir-ee; we want to visit the school. Hooray, here's Florence, the smart Florence! What a beauty!" and Roy snatched up that beloved pupil by the head and whirled her around so rudely that her delicate neck snapped in two.

"I hope you feel satisfied now," said Millie, with an awful calmness.

"I say, girls," said Ralph, "let's have a good game of 'Hy Spy.' Let your old school go. You can play that any time. Come on, and have some fun."

Both the girls being very fond of "Hy Spy," they concluded to forego their wrath for the present, and join in the game.

—MARY PRUDENCE WELLS SMITH.

A BOY'S SONG

ha'zel   ban'ter   clus'ter ing

Where the pools are bright and deep,
Where the gray trout lies asleep,
Up the river and o'er the lea,
That's the way for Billy and me.

Where the blackbird sings the latest,
Where the hawthorn blooms the sweetest,

Where the nestlings chirp and flee,
That's the way for Billy and me.

Where the mowers mow the cleanest,
Where the hay lies thick and greenest;
There to trace the homeward bee,
That's the way for Billy and me.

Where the hazel bank is steepest,
Where the shadow falls the deepest,
Where the clustering nuts fall free,
That's the way for Billy and me.

Why the boys should drive away
Little sweet maidens from their play,
Or love to banter and fight so well,
That's the thing I never could tell.

But this I know, I love to play,
Through the meadow, among the hay;
Up the water and o'er the lea,
That's the way for Billy and me.

— James Hogg.

CERES AND PROSERPINE

Ce'res   Ju'pi ter   Mer'cu ry   pome gran'ate
A pol'lo char'i ot Plu'to   Pro ser'pi ne

Once upon a time there was a goddess named Ceres. She had the care of the flowers and the fruits.

Ceres had a dear little daughter named Proserpine.

Proserpine spent her days in the fields. She loved to gather lilies and violets and to make wreaths for her friends.

One day Proserpine and her little friends

were playing happily in the meadow. A short distance off they saw a strange and wonderful flower. It had one hundred bells on its tall stalk.

"Oh, see!" cried Proserpine, "I must have that flower." And she ran to pluck it.

Suddenly the ground shook and trembled. Then it yawned before her. From the depths of the earth came a dark chariot drawn by six coal-black horses.

A king with a dark brow and an iron crown held the reins. He seized little Proserpine, and before she could cry for help, he disappeared with her back into the earth.

After a time the other children missed Proserpine. They thought she must be hiding.

They searched, but failed to find her. Then they told Ceres.

Ceres was heart-broken when she heard that her little girl was lost. She dressed herself in black from head to foot, took a torch in her hand, and went out searching for her little daughter.

Just think how your mother would feel if you were lost!

Ceres walked till she came to a cottage. An old woman sat at the door. She was the goddess of the moon.

Ceres said, " Surely you know where my daughter is ! " But the goddess of the moon answered, " Alas, no ! "

Ceres went on her lonely way, till she reached the shore of a lake. There sat a fair young man. He was Apollo, the god of the sun.

Ceres said again, " Surely you know where my daughter is ! "

Apollo looked into her sad face and had pity on her. " Yes," he replied, " I do know where your daughter is. Pluto has taken her to his palace in the underworld."

Ceres walked on till she came to a fountain. By its edge she seated herself. She buried her face in her hands and wept aloud. "Shall I ever see my Proserpine again?" she cried.

Two girls came along with pitchers on their heads. They asked her why she grieved. When she had told them, they said, " Come and live with us, and we will make you as happy as we can."

Ceres dwelt with them one year. But during that time, her heart grew harder and harder. She was angry with the earth for opening to let Pluto pass with Proserpine. So she cursed the ground. " Wicked soil," she cried, " cease to be fruitful ! "

Immediately the grass and flowers withered ; the good seed failed to come up ; the cattle died ; and even man grew ill and unhappy.

At last Jupiter heard the cries of man. " This distress must cease," he said ; and he sent for Ceres.

He listened to her sad story and promised her help. Mercury was sent to the underworld with this message: "Restore Proserpine at once to her mother."

Now Pluto loved Proserpine and had made her his queen. .Day by day he urged her to eat, and day by day she refused. Pluto knew that if she would but eat, even the smallest morsel, she was his.

For nine months Proserpine had eaten nothing. But one day she was tempted by the sweet pulp of a pomegranate. She ate it, and Pluto was happy.

He knew now that, even should she return to Ceres, she must spend part of the year with him.

Soon Mercury came to take Proserpine to her mother.

Ceres heard the rustle of Proserpine's dress. She looked up. There stood her dearly loved daughter.

She clasped her in her arms, crying, "Now we shall live happily together forever."

" That cannot be, mother," answered Proserpine. " Pluto gave me an enchanted fruit before I came away. In six months' time I must return to him again."

How happy Ceres was while her daughter was with her! The gay flowers and grass grew once more upon the earth.

But, even to-day, during the long six months that Proserpine spends in the underworld, no green thing comes up out of the ground.

—FANNY E. COE.

THE LOST DOLL

I once had a sweet little doll, dears,
   The prettiest doll in the world;
Her cheeks were so red and so white, dears,
   And her hair was so charmingly curled.

But I lost my poor little doll, dears,
   As I played on the heath one day;
And I cried for more than a week, dears,
   But I never could find where she lay.

I found my poor little doll, dears,
  As I played on the heath one day;
Folks say she is terribly changed, dears,
  For her paint is all washed away.

And her arms trodden off by the cows, dears,
  And her hair's not the least bit curled;
Yet for old time's sake, she is still, dears,
  The prettiest doll in the world.

                    —Charles Kingsley.

THE PETERKINS AT DINNER

in'ci dent	Pe'ter kin	veg'e ta bles
dif'fi cul ty	pre ferred'	Sol'o mon
Ag a mem'non	in'dia-rub'ber	

This little incident happened in the Peterkin family. It was at dinner time.

They sat down to a dish of boiled ham. Now half the children liked fat and half liked lean. Mr. Peterkin sat down to cut the ham. But the ham was a very unusual one. The fat and the lean came in separate slices,—first one of lean, then one of fat, and so on.

Mr. Peterkin began by helping the children according to their age. Now Agamemnon who liked lean, got a fat slice; and Elizabeth Eliza who preferred fat, had a lean slice. Solomon John, who could eat nothing but lean, was helped to fat, and so on. None had what he could eat.

It was a rule of the Peterkin family that no one should eat vegetables without meat. Although the children saw upon their plates apple sauce, squash, and sweet potato, no one could take a mouthful, because no one was satisfied with his meat.

Mr. and Mrs. Peterkin, however, liked both fat and lean. They were making a good meal, when they looked up and saw the children eating nothing.

"What is the matter?" said Mr. Peterkin.

But the children had been taught not to speak at table. Agamemnon, however, made a sign of disgust at his fat, and Elizabeth Eliza at her lean. So the parents understood the difficulty.

"What shall be done now?" said Mrs. Peterkin. They all sat and thought for a while.

At last Mrs. Peterkin said, "Suppose we ask the lady from Philadelphia what is best to be done."

But Mr. Peterkin said he didn't like to go to her for everything; let the children try to eat their dinner as it was.

They all tried, but they couldn't.

"Very well, then," said Mrs. Peterkin, "let them go and ask the lady from Philadelphia."

"All of us?" cried one of the little boys.

"Yes," said Mrs. Peterkin, "only put on your india-rubber boots." And they hurried out of the house.

The lady from Philadelphia was just going in to her dinner, but she kindly stopped in the entry to hear what the trouble was. After Agamemnon and Elizabeth Eliza had told her, she said, "But why don't you give the slices of fat to those who like the fat, and the slices of lean to those who like the lean?"

They all looked at one another. Agamemnon looked at Elizabeth Eliza, and Solomon John looked at the little boys.

"Why didn't we think of that?" said they; and they ran to tell their mother.

— LUCRETIA P. HALE.

HOW THE CRICKETS BROUGHT GOOD FORTUNE

re quest'   re ceived'   Jacques   re ceipt'ed

My friend Jacques went into a baker's shop one day to buy a little cake. He meant it for a sick child who could be coaxed to eat only by tempting his appetite.

While he waited for his change, a little boy in poor but clean clothes entered the shop.

"Ma'am," said he to the baker's wife, "mother sent me for a loaf of bread."

The woman took from the shelf the best loaf she could find and put it into the arms of the boy.

"Have you any money?" said the baker's wife.

The little boy's eyes grew sad.

"No, ma'am," said he, hugging the loaf closer to his thin jacket, "but mother told me to say that she would come to-morrow to speak to you about it."

"Run along," said the kind woman; "carry your bread home, child."

"Thank you, ma'am," said the poor little fellow.

My friend Jacques now received his purchase and change and turned to go. He found the child, whom he had supposed to be halfway home, standing stock-still behind him.

"What are you doing there?" asked the baker's wife. "Don't you like the bread?"

"Oh, yes, ma'am!"

"Well, then, carry it to your mother, my little friend. If you wait any longer, you will get a scolding."

The child did not seem to hear. Something else held his attention.

The baker's wife went to him and tapped him gently on the shoulder. "What *are* you thinking about?" said she.

" Ma'am," said the little boy, " what is it that sings ? "

"There is no singing."

" Yes ! " cried the little fellow. " Hear it ! Queek, queek, queek, queek ! "

My friend and the woman both listened but heard only the chirp of the crickets. These little creatures are often guests in bakers' houses.

" It is a little bird," said the dear little fellow, " or perhaps the bread sings when it bakes, as apples do."

" No, indeed, little goose ! " said the baker's wife. " Those are crickets. They sing because we are lighting the oven and they like to see the fire."

" Ma'am," said the child, blushing at his bold request, " I should be so happy if you would give me a cricket."

" A cricket ! What in the world would you do with a cricket, my dear ? I would gladly give you all there are in the house to get rid of them."

"Oh, ma'am, give me one, only one, if you please!" cried the child, clasping his thin little hands under the big loaf. "They say that crickets bring good luck. Perhaps if we had one at home, mother wouldn't cry any more."

"Why does your poor mother cry?" asked Jacques.

"Because of her bills, sir. Father is dead, and mother works very hard, but she cannot pay them all."

My friend took the child, and with him the great loaf, into his arms, and I really believe he kissed them both.

Meanwhile the baker's wife had gone into the bakehouse. She made her husband catch four crickets. These he put into a box with a hole in the cover, so that they might breathe.

Then the woman gave them to the happy child.

When he had gone, the baker's wife took down the account book and found the page where the mother's charges were written. She made a great dash down the leaf and wrote at the bottom, *Paid.*

Meanwhile Jacques had wrapped in paper all the money he had found in his pockets.

Then he wrote a note to the mother of the little cricket boy, telling her she had a son who would one day be her pride and joy.

The money, the note, and the receipted bill they gave to a baker's boy with long legs. " Hurry now! " said they.

The child, with his big loaf, his four crickets, and his little short legs could not run very fast. The baker's boy reached the house first.

Thus the child found his mother, for the first time in weeks, resting from her work with a happy smile upon her lips.

" Oh, the crickets have done it ! " he cried, and I do not think he was mistaken. With- out the crickets and his good little heart, would this blessed change have taken place in his mother's fortune ?

—From the French of P. J. STAHL.

THE STORY OF THE *BIRKENHEAD*

col'o nel   tre men'dous   lieu ten'ant

A great ship sailed out of Queenstown Harbor. There were over six hundred souls on board. Most of these were soldiers on their way to fight for their queen in South Africa.

Many of these soldiers were under twenty. Some were fresh from the farm; others had just left school. They were under the command of Lieutenant Colonel Seton.

Besides the soldiers and the sailors, there were on board many women and children. They were the wives and little ones of the soldiers.

The children led a gay life at sea. They played about the decks by day, and at night slept as sweetly as if they had been in their cradles at home. Day after day, kind winds blew them steadily south. Night after night, the kind ocean rocked them to sleep.

One fine, starlight night there came a tremendous crash. All awoke and rushed on deck. They learned that the ship had struck on a rock and that they were in great danger.

Boats were lowered. But alas! there were not enough for all. Who should go?

The women and children were put into the boats with a few sailors to row them. Land was near and the sea was calm. They probably would be saved.

(38)   ''Colonel Seton drew them up in battle array.''

As the boats moved off, the captain cried, " All who can swim, go with the boats! "

But Colonel Seton said, "Men, stay here! Would you risk the lives of the women and children?" And not a man stirred. They saw that even so few as two or three more men in each boat would overturn it.

And now they faced death. Colonel Seton drew them up in battle array. Overhead waved the English flag. The old soldiers and the lads stood shoulder to shoulder. Their faces were white, but their eyes were steady, and their lips firm.

So, with its deckful of heroes the *Birkenhead* sank from sight.

There was mourning in England, but there was a proud joy too. England felt herself the richer by those heroes of the *Birkenhead*.

—FANNY E. COE.

GOOD NIGHT AND GOOD MORNING

cu'ri ous   courte'sied   neighed

A fair little girl sat under a tree,
Sewing as long as her eyes could see;
Then smoothed her work and folded it right,
And said, "Dear work, good night, good
    night!"

Such a number of rooks came over her head,
Crying, "Caw! Caw!" on their way to bed,
She said, as she watched their curious flight,
"Little black things, good night, good night!"

The horses neighed, and the oxen lowed,
The sheep's "Bleat! Bleat!" came over the
    road,
All seeming to say, with a quiet delight,
"Good little girl, good night, good night!"

She did not say to the sun, "Good night!"
Though she saw him there like a ball of light;
For she knew he had God's own time to keep
All over the world, and never could sleep.

The tall pink foxglove bowed his head;
The violets courtesied, and went to bed;
And good little Lucy tied up her hair,
And said, on her knees, her favorite prayer.

And, while on her pillow she softly lay,
She knew nothing more till again it was day;
And all things said to the beautiful sun,
"Good morning, good morning! our work is
    begun."

       —Lord Houghton.

GRACE DARLING

dis tress'   ten'der ly   neigh'bor ing

Grace Darling was an English girl who lived in a lighthouse. This lighthouse stood on a lonely island off the English coast. The lamp was tended by Grace's father.

Mr. Darling was now an old man, but he and Grace lived quite alone. Grace was strong and skillful. She could row a boat as well as a man.

One night there came on a terrible gale. The winds blew fiercely and the sea beat high against the lighthouse tower. It was long before the Darlings fell asleep.

Suddenly Grace awoke. She thought she had heard a cry. She sprang to the window and looked out. It was too dark as yet to see, but again and again there floated across the water sharp cries of distress.

When dawn came, Grace woke her father and together they went down upon the shore.

A large steamer was lying wrecked upon a neighboring island.

"Father," said Grace, "we must launch a boat. Some people are on that wreck."

But Mr. Darling shook his head. The wind blew fearfully; the tide too was rising. To launch a boat meant certain death.

Grace saw an arm waved from the wreck.

"Father, some one is still alive out there. I must go." She pushed off the boat and sprang in.

Her father would not let his daughter face death alone. He leaped into the boat also.

Often the frail boat nearly upset. Storm and spray beat against their faces, but steadily they drew nearer the wreck.

At length Grace could count nine persons clinging to the side of the steamer. One by one these nine persons were taken into the boat. Then Grace and her father rowed them ashore.

For several days Grace cared for them tenderly. Then the storm passed and they were able to return home.

The story of the courage of Grace Darling was told all through England. Many rich gifts were sent her, but what she cared for most was the joy of having done her duty.

— FANNY E. COE.

LITTLE RED RIDING–HOOD

bob'bin   cau'tion   muf'fled

Once upon a time there was a little girl. She lived with her mother in a cottage on the edge of a wood. On the other side of the wood lived her grandmother.

This dear old lady had made her grandchild a pretty red cloak and hood which she was seldom seen without. On this account she was called Little Red Riding-hood.

One day her mother called Little Red Riding-hood and put a basket into her hand.

"I wish you to go to your grandmother's, dear, and see how she is. I hear she has been ill. Give her the cake and the little pot of butter that are in the basket. Don't stop to play by the way, and don't talk to any one you may meet."

Little Red Riding-hood hurried along the path to her grandmother's. Halfway through the wood, she met a great wolf. He wished to eat her, but dared not because some wood choppers were working near by; so he began to talk to her instead. " Where are you going, little girl ?" he asked.

Red Riding-hood forgot her mother's caution. " I am going to see my grandmother," she replied. " In my basket are a cake and a little pot of butter from my mother."

" Does she live far off ? " asked the wolf.

" Oh, yes. It is the first house in the village after you pass the mill."

" I think," said the wolf, " that I will go to see your grandmother too. I will go this way, and you, that, and we shall see who will get there first."

The sly wolf took the nearest way and Red Riding-hood went by the farthest. The wolf raced all the way, while the little girl idled along in the bright sunshine. Sometimes too, she stopped to pick flowers or to chase a butterfly; so the wolf reached the grandmother's first.

Tap, tap, tap! came his knock at the door.

" Who is there ? "

" Your grandchild, Little Red Riding-hood. Mother has sent me with a cake and a little pot of butter."

The good grandmother, who was ill in bed, called out, " Pull the bobbin and the latch will fly up."

The wolf did as he was told and the door opened. Into the cottage sprang the fierce animal. He leaped upon the bed and ate up the old woman in no time, for he had gone three days without food.

" Now for Little Red Riding-hood," thought the wolf. He put on the grandmother's nightdress and cap and got into bed.

"She met a great wolf."

Very soon there came a gentle tap, tap at the door.

"Who is there?"

The big voice frightened Red Riding-hood at first. Then she said to herself, "Grandmother must have a bad cold." So she replied, "This is Little Red Riding-hood. Mother has sent you a cake and a little pot of butter."

"Pull the bobbin and the latch will go up," said the wolf, in his softest voice.

Little Red Riding-hood pulled the bobbin, and the latch flew up and the door opened.

The wolf hid under the bedclothes and said in a muffled voice, "Now, dear, put the cake and the pot of butter on the shelf and come to bed."

Little Red Riding-hood made ready for bed. Then she came to the bedside and gazed with wonder at her grandmother.

"Grandmother, what great arms you have!"

"The better to hug you, my dear."

" Grandmother, what great ears you have ! "

" The better to hear you, my dear."

" Grandmother, what great eyes you have ! "

" The better to see you, my dear."

" Oh, Grandmother, what great teeth you have ! "

" The better to eat you, my dear."

With these words the wicked wolf sprang out of bed and ate up poor Little Red Riding-hood.

But the little girl's cries had been heard by a woodcutter. With ax in hand he hastened to the cottage.

The wicked wolf sprang upon the man as he entered the door. But the woodcutter was the stronger.

With one blow of his ax he cut open the wicked wolf and lo ! a wonderful thing happened. Red Riding-hood and her grandmother, alive and well, stood before him.

How glad they were to thank the kind woodcutter who had saved their lives !

THE PETERKINS GO TO DRIVE

min'is ter   thought'ful ly   op'e ra glass
Twom'ly   ex act'ly   neigh'bors

One morning Mrs. Peterkin was feeling very tired. She said to Mr. Peterkin, " I believe I shall take a ride this morning!"

The little boys cried out, " Oh, may we go too?"

Mrs. Peterkin said that Elizabeth Eliza and the little boys might go.

Mr. Peterkin had the horse put into the carryall, and he and Agamemnon went off to their business. Solomon John went to school, and Mrs. Peterkin began to get ready for her drive.

She had some currants she wanted to carry to old Mrs. Twomly and some gooseberries for somebody else. Elizabeth Eliza wanted to pick some flowers to take to the minister's wife. So it took them a long time to prepare.

The little boys went out to pick the currants and the gooseberries, and Elizabeth Eliza went out for her flowers. Mrs. Peterkin put on her cape-bonnet and in time they were all ready. The little boys were in their india-rubber boots and they got into the carriage.

Elizabeth Eliza was to drive. She sat on the front seat and took up the reins, and the horse started off merrily. Then he suddenly stopped and would not go any farther.

Elizabeth Eliza shook the reins, and pulled them. Then she clucked to the horse. Mrs. Peterkin clucked. The little boys whistled and shouted. Still the horse would not go.

"We shall have to whip him," said Elizabeth Eliza.

Now Mrs. Peterkin never liked to use the whip. She said she would get out and turn her head the other way, while Elizabeth Eliza whipped the horse. When he began to go, she would hurry and get in.

They tried this, but the horse would not stir. "Perhaps we have too heavy a load," said Mrs. Peterkin, as she got in.

So they took out the currants, and the gooseberries, and the flowers, but still the horse would not go.

One of the neighbors looking out just then called out to them to try the whip.

"I have tried the whip," said Elizabeth Eliza.

"She says 'whips' such as you eat," said one of the little boys.

"We might make those," said Mrs. Peterkin, thoughtfully.

"We have plenty of cream," said Elizabeth Eliza.

"Yes, let us have some whips," cried the little boys.

So they went into the kitchen, and whipped up the cream, and made some very delicious whips. The little boys tasted all round, and every one thought they were very nice.

They carried some out to the horse who swallowed it down very quickly.

"That is just what he wanted," said Mrs. Peterkin. "Now he will certainly go!"

Then all got into the carriage again, and put in the currants and the gooseberries and the flowers. Elizabeth Eliza shook the reins and they all clucked. Still the horse would not go!

"We must either give up our ride," said Mrs. Peterkin, "or else send over to the lady from Philadelphia, and see what she will say."

The little boys jumped out as quickly as they could. They were eager to go to ask the lady from Philadelphia. Elizabeth Eliza went with them, while her mother took the reins.

They found the lady from Philadelphia very ill that day. She was in bed.

When she was told what the trouble was, she very kindly said they might open the blinds at the foot of the bed, and she would see. Then she asked for her opera glass, and looked through it, up the street to Mrs. Peterkin's door.

After she had looked through the glass, she leaned her head back against the pillow, for she was very tired. Then she said, "Why don't you unchain the horse from the horse post?"

Elizabeth Eliza and the little boys looked at one another. Then they hurried back to the house and told their mother. The horse was untied, and they all went to ride.

— Lucretia P. Hale.

55

THE LITTLE MIDSHIPMAN

mid'ship man O'ri ent ex plo'sion

dis ap peared' Cas a bi an'ca prom' ise

The battle was about to begin. The French had seventeen ships and the English but fourteen. The largest ship of all was a French one. It had three decks and one hundred and twenty guns. Its name was the *Orient*.

The flag captain had his little son on board. The boy was a midshipman and was about ten years old. This would be his first battle.

His father, Captain Casabianca, wished to place his son in safety. He stationed him on the upper deck. "Stay here, my boy, whatever happens. Stay here till father comes for you," he said.

"I will, sir," replied the lad.

For hours the battle raged. The day was going against the French. Suddenly the *Orient* caught fire. There was great danger for all on board, as there was much powder in the hold.

The sailors lowered the boats. "Come, little Casabianca," they called, "come with us!"

But the boy shook his head. "I must wait till father tells me to go," he cried. Poor boy! he did not know that an English shot had killed his father an hour before.

And now, the very last boat is leaving. "Come, Casabianca," the sailors call. "Here is the last chance to save your life! Come! Come!"

"Father, O father!" the boy calls, "may I go? *Must* I stay?"

No voice replies, and the gallant lad, true to his promise, waves his hand in farewell to the sailors. They watch him sadly as they row away.

Suddenly there is a terrible explosion. The powder has taken fire and the ship *Orient* has disappeared. The little midshipman was faithful unto death.

—FANNY E. COE.

CASABIANCA

he ro'ic   un con'scious   pen'non   chief'tain
splen'dor frag'ments   shroud   wreath'ing

The boy stood on the burning deck
    Whence all but him had fled;
The flame that lit the battle's wreck
    Shone round him o'er the dead.

Yet beautiful and bright he stood,
    As born to rule the storm —
A creature of heroic blood
    A proud, though childlike form.

The flames rolled on, — he would not go
    Without his father's word;
That father, faint in death below,
    His voice no longer heard.

He called aloud, "Say, father, say
    If yet my task is done!"
He knew not that the chieftain lay
    Unconscious of his son.

" Speak, father ! " once again he cried,
  " If I may yet be gone ! "
And but the booming shots replied,
  And fast the flames rolled on.

Upon his brow he felt their breath,
  And in his waving hair,
And looked from that lone post of death
  In still, yet brave despair;

And shouted but once more aloud,
  " My father ! must I stay ? "
While o'er him fast, through sail and
    shroud,
  The wreathing fires made way.

They wrapped the ship in splendor wild,
  They caught the flag on high,
And streamed above the gallant child
  Like banners in the sky.

Then came a burst of thunder sound —
  The boy — oh ! where was he ?
Ask of the winds that far around
  With fragments strewed the sea,

With mast, and helm, and pennon fair,
That well had borne their part;
But the noblest thing that perished there
Was that young faithful heart!
— FELICIA HEMANS.

THE QUEEN BEE

en chant'ed   pres'ent ly   Dumm'ling

Once upon a time there lived three king's
sons. I never heard the names of the two
elder sons, but the youngest was called
Dummling. This was because all thought
him a simple, foolish fellow.

In time the two elder sons went out to seek
their fortunes. Years passed, but no word
from them came back to their father.

One day the old king said, "Dummling,
it is time you were starting out in the world.
Perhaps you may at least find your brothers."

Dummling did find them after a time.
They were poor as ever. How they jeered
when Dummling said he had come to seek his

fortune! But they all three went on together till they came to an ant-hill.

" What sport ! " cried the eldest. " Let us stir up this ant-hill. "

" Yes," said the second brother. " It will be jolly sport to see the ants carrying off their eggs."

But Dummling stepped before them, saying,

"Leave the poor little ants alone. I will not let you harm them."

Further on they came to a lake, where a number of ducks were swimming about.

"Let us catch a few," said the eldest.

"Yes, and roast them," added the second brother. "I was always fond of roast duck."

But Dummling cried, "Leave the ducks alone. I will not let you kill them."

Presently they came to a bees' nest in a tree. The bees had stored so much honey that it overflowed and ran down the trunk.

"How I like honey!" cried the eldest. "But the bees would sting us badly, should we try to get it."

"Let us build a fire under the tree," said the second brother. "The smoke will stifle the bees, and then we can get the honey with ease."

But a third time Dummling stood in their way. "Leave the poor bees alone. I will not let you stifle them."

At last the three brothers came to an enchanted castle. They went through the great rooms till finally they stood before a door fastened with three bolts. In the middle of the door was a small window through which they peeped.

They saw a small, gray-haired man sitting at a table. They called to him several times, but he did not hear. At last Dummling called alone and the small man heard. He undid the bolts and came out.

Silently he led them to a table spread with delicious food. When they had finished their meal, he led them each to a bedroom.

In the morning the small man awoke the eldest brother. He led him to a table of stone on which was some writing. The writing told of the three tasks by which the castle could be freed from its enchantment.

The eldest brother read thus: " Under the moss in the castle forest are hidden the pearls of the princess. They number one thousand. He who would free the castle from its spell must first collect these. If he who undertakes to gather them has not finished his task by sunset, — if but one pearl is missing, — he must be turned to stone."

The eldest brother went to the forest and searched all day. But at sunset he had found only one hundred pearls; so he was turned to stone.

Next morning the small gray man awoke the second brother and led him also to the table of stone. The second brother undertook the task, but he fared very little better than the first. He collected but two hundred pearls, and so, at sunset, he also was turned to stone.

Now came Dummling's turn. He began to search in the moss, but he soon lost heart. Sitting down on a stone, he began to weep. While he was weeping, the ant king with five thousand ants came to his help. Soon these tiny creatures had gathered all the pearls into a beautiful shining heap at Dummling's feet.

"Thank you, thank you, dear ants," he said. "You have saved my life."

"You saved our lives, Dummling, a few days ago. We never forget our friends."

Next morning Dummling read on the stone table: "He who would free the castle from enchantment must find the key of the Prin-

cess's sleeping room in the depths of the castle lake."

Dummling walked down to the castle lake and his heart was heavy. The lake was

miles across. "If I should dive a dozen times an hour from now till sunset, I should never find that key. By six to-night I too shall be stone."

He was about to weep when suddenly a company of ducks came swimming towards him. Again and again they stopped to dive. Soon one swam towards him with a large golden key in his bill.

"Thank you, thank you, dear ducks," cried Dummling. "You have saved my life."

"You saved our lives, Dummling, a few days ago. We never forget our friends."

The third morning Dummling read the last and hardest task on the stone table: "In the room opened by the golden key three princesses lie asleep. Before resting, each had eaten a different sweetmeat, — the eldest a lump of sugar; the second, a little sirup; and the third, a spoonful of honey. He who would free the castle must choose the youngest and loveliest of the three."

As Dummling entered the room he thought

that his task was hopeless. The princesses were exactly alike and so dazzling in their beauty that the poor youth could scarcely look at them. "At last I shall fail," he thought.

Just then, through the open window came flying the Queen Bee. Dummling held his breath, as he watched her. She lighted on the rosy lips of each princess in turn. Finally she settled on the lips of her who had eaten the honey.

"Thank you, thank you, dear Queen Bee," cried Dummling. "You have saved my life."

"You saved our lives, Dummling, a few days ago. We bee people never forget our friends."

Then Dummling took the youngest princess by the hand and at once the spell was broken. All awoke from their stony sleep. The two brothers also took their right form again.

Dummling married the youngest princess and became king of the country. His two brothers married the two other sisters, but stayed princes all their lives.

LITTLE MAY

blos'somed   drow'sy   re peat'

Have you heard the waters singing,
    Little May,
Where the willows green are bending
    O'er their way?

Do you know how low and sweet,
O'er the pebbles at their feet,
Are the words the waves repeat,
    Night and day?

Have you heard the robins singing,
    Little one,
When the rosy dawn is breaking, —
    When 'tis done?
Have you heard the wooing breeze,
In the blossomed orchard trees,
And the drowsy hum of bees
    In the sun?

All the earth is full of music,
    Little May, —
Bird, and bee, and water singing
    On its way.
Let their silver voices fall
On thy heart with happy call:
"Praise the Lord who loveth all,"
    Night and day,
    Little May.

    — EMILY HUNTINGTON MILLER.

A NIGHT'S ADVENTURE ON THE OHIO RIVER

AN INCIDENT OF THE FLOOD OF 1832

com pre hend'ed	Cin cin na'ti	sur round'ed
dis tinct'ly	en cour'aged	pro ceed'ed
a void'ing	crouched	· ref'uge
ap peared'	ex er'tions	ex pect'ed

"The river rises fast, wife," said Jack Martin. "It is almost up to the top of the bank now."

"Do you think there is any danger?" asked Mrs. Martin.

"No; the river will go down as it came up, when it is ready. Come in!"

A boy of thirteen appeared at the door.

"Mother is sick, Mrs. Martin," he said, "and she sent me to ask you to come over."

"Well, I expected it," said Mrs. Martin. "What shall I do?"

"Go, of course," said her husband. "I will put Dolly into the wagon and we will go by the upper road and take the doctor in."

"But the children, father."

"Now, don't worry, Molly. Sally can take care of the baby, and I shall not be gone more than an hour. You can get along, can't you, Sally?"

"I think so," was the smiling reply of a bright-eyed girl of thirteen.

After her parents had gone, Sally proceeded to wash up the tea things. Will, a boy of nine, got out his slate and arithmetic and began to cipher.

Thus an hour passed. The baby awoke and was fed. Then the older children prepared for bed.

Usually they slept in the loft, but to-night they had been told to sleep below with the baby. They rolled a large log on the fire and put a candle in the lantern, before undressing. Soon after they were sound asleep.

Suddenly Sally was awakened by she knew not what. There was a groaning, creaking noise, and she thought she felt the house move.

Without waking William, she sprang out upon the floor and ran toward the fireplace.

As she reached it her feet splashed in water. Quick as light the thought came, "The river is up!" She groped for a candle, touched it to a coal, and had a light.

A quick glance told her what was the matter. The hearth had sunk several inches below the floor of the room. Up through the crevices came the water.

Raising the window curtain, Sally gazed out. The house was surrounded by water. The waves were washing up against it and over the doorstep. As far as her eyes could see was water, only water, with trees standing in it.

Running to the bed, she shook Will. "Get up, Will, get up! The river is all around the house." The boy sat up, rubbed his eyes, and then sank back again. "Get up, Will, do get up! Don't you hear? The river is coming into the house!"

Will comprehended at last, and while putting on his clothes, ran to the window.

"What are we to do?" he asked. "If father were only here!"

"We must go to the loft and wait until father comes," she answered.

Taking the baby in her arms, she climbed the stairway and laid it on her bed. Then they carried to the loft all the articles they could move, not forgetting some bread and a crock of milk for the baby. They then took refuge there themselves.

Wrapped in comforters, they held each other close, not daring to go to bed. They crouched near one of the windows. It was not a dark night, and they could see that the water spread over the meadows almost to the hills.

The little wooden clock on the mantel shelf below struck two. Soon after there was a great noise, as of something tearing away, — a jarring and a jerking. The house swayed to and fro and went down one side and up the other. The children covered up their heads and clung closer to each other.

A moment more and all was quiet again. Presently Sally stood up and said, "We are moving, Will; the house is moving!"

She ran to the front window and looked out. They were afloat on the broad Ohio.

Will saw the terror in Sally's face. Clinging close to her, he said softly, " Don't cry, Sally! God will help us."

Somewhat herself again, Sally took the baby up and fed it. Then she crept to the window again with Will.

" It will soon be morning," he said.

" Then the people will see us and come to take us away," was her reply.

The clock had struck four. Dark objects went swiftly by them. Every little while the house would dip and rock, as a log or tree struck it.

Five o'clock struck, and then six. They began to see objects distinctly in the dawning light.

" See," cried Will, " there is a coop full of chickens ! "

" There is a dog house turned upside down and the poor dog is clinging to the outside with his paws. He is chained to it."

"Oh!" Some large object had struck the house and the children were thrown upon the floor.

With the light, all Sally's energy came back to her. Taking the sheets off the bed, she fastened them to a couple óf slats which she nailed to the window sill. This was what she had seen people do on the river bank when they wished a steamboat to stop.

An hour passed. Sally was almost frantic. She had seen people making signals to them, but none came to help.

"We are coming to a town. This must be Cincinnati. See the houses!" Sally leaned out the window, shrieking for aid.

"Put the baby down, Will, and come and wave," she said. Will obeyed.

"They see us! Why don't they help us! It is Cincinnati! See the boats!"

People saw and shouted to them, but seemed to have no power to reach them. The children increased their exertions, encouraged by the knowledge that they were seen. Sally brought the baby from the bed and held it up.

Presently a large boat came towards them. Slowly and steadily it moved in and out, avoiding the driftwood float-  ing by. A few lengths and it would be beside the house.

Just then a huge saw log was struck by something and dashed into the side of the dwell- ing. A shriek was given by the lookers-on as the children disappeared. By a few clever strokes the boat gained the side of the ruin. One of the crew climbed to the window where the children had again appeared, and lifted them out. A moment more and the house fell over on its side.

"I thought God would take care of us," whispered Will to Sally.

— MARTHA M. THOMAS.

WE ARE SEVEN

ker'chief   por'rin ger   rus'tic

A simple child,
That lightly draws its breath,
And feels its life in every limb,
What should it know of death?

I met a little cottage girl;
She was eight years old, she said;
Her hair was thick with many a curl
That clustered round her head.

She had a rustic, woodland air,
And she was wildly clad:
Her eyes were fair, and very fair;
— Her beauty made me glad.

" Sisters and brothers, little maid,
How many may you be ? "

" How many ? Seven in all,"
  she said,
And wondering, looked at
  me.

" And where are they ?   I pray you tell."
She answered, " Seven are we ;
And two of us at Conway dwell,
And two are gone to sea.

" Two of us in the churchyard lie,
My sister and my brother;
And, in the churchyard cottage, I
Dwell near them with my mother."

" You say that two at Conway dwell,
And two are gone to sea,
Yet ye are seven! — I pray you tell,
Sweet maid, how this may be."

Then did the little maid reply,
" Seven boys and girls are we;
Two of us in the churchyard lie
Beneath the churchyard tree."

" You run about, my little maid,
Your limbs they are alive;
If two are in the churchyard laid,
Then ye are only five."

" Their graves are green, they may be seen,"
The little maid replied;
" Twelve steps or more from my mother's
    door,
And they are side by side.

" My stockings there I often knit,
My kerchief there I hem ;
And there upon the ground I sit,
And sing a song to them.

" And often after sunset, Sir,
When it is light and fair,
I take my little porringer,
And eat my supper there.

" The first that died was little Jane ;
In bed she moaning lay,
Till God released her of her pain,
And then she went away.

" So in the churchyard she was laid ;
And, when the grass was dry,
Together round her grave we played,
My brother John and I.

" And when the ground was white with snow,
And I could run and slide,
My brother John was forced to go,
And he lies by her side."

"How many are you then," said I,
" If they two are in heaven ? "
Quick was the little maid's reply,
" O Master! we are seven."

" But they are dead; those two are dead!
Their spirits are in heaven! "
'Twas throwing words away; for still
The little maid would have her will,
And said, " Nay, we are seven! "

—WILLIAM WORDSWORTH.

SIGNS OF BABY

rum'ble	dis cov'ered	cu'ri ous
Er'ic	lul'la by	plain'tive
plen'ti ful	aft'er noons'	with'er ing

The last half of a long drive always seems
much longer than the first. That is what the
children were thinking as they sat, tired and
silent, in grandfather's big wagon, and wondered why the railway station was so far from
the farm. But away in the western plains of
America, railways are not so plentiful as they

are with us; houses, too, are sometimes few and far between.

Katie gave a big sigh that was heard even above the rumble of the wagon, as they passed a bare little wooden house, rough and unpainted. Then mamma said in a cheery voice, just as if she were not a bit tired, "There's a baby in that house."

"Where? I don't see one," said Eric.

"Look at the clothesline," said mamma, laughing. "On Monday afternoons I can

always tell a house where there is a baby, for all the little clothes are hanging out from the wash. I feel sorry for a house where I don't see signs of Baby."

"Why, I never thought of looking," said Kate.

"Nor I," said Eric.

COE'S THIRD R. — 6

Grandfather laughed quietly. " I'm seventy years old, and *I* never looked. I'm going to begin now."

At the next house they passed there were no clothes on the line; but grandfather nodded his gray head and remarked, " There's a baby in that house."

" Why, I don't see a sign of one," said Eric.

" I see a sign," grandfather said; and he let the horses walk slowly past the house.

Then Katie saw it. " There's a board nailed across the kitchen door to keep him from tumbling out," she cried; and just then a round, curly head with two big brown eyes appeared above the board.

" Oh," said Eric, " there he is, sure enough; I was looking for his clothes!"

It was great fun after that watching all the houses for signs of a baby.

" Listen! There's a baby in there," said mamma, as they passed a bright new house, and from the open door they heard a low, sweet lullaby sung by a woman's voice.

"Yes, there's a baby," said the children. —
"Drive gently, grandfather; he's just going
to sleep. We must not wake him up again."

At another house grandfather discovered a
sign, and such a
curious one that
even mother
could not find
it.

"Are you
sure, grand-
father?" Eric
asked.

"Yes, I see
it," was all he
said; and he let
the horses stop
for a drink,
while the others
looked and searched with keen eyes.

"We give it up; you must tell us," they
said at last. And then he pointed with his
whip to a bed of gay poppies where little

heaps of the bright blossoms were lying at the side withering in the sun.

"Are you *sure* about that sign?" Eric asked.

"Yes, quite sure. What a little rogue he is, too, to pluck all those flowers!" said grandfather. "But if you won't believe my sign, there's another," he went on. And this time he pointed to a little straw hat lying by the roadside with a handful of withered flowers beside it.

It was Eric who discovered the last sign of all as they drew near the end of the drive. They were passing a pretty little home with a pleasant garden in front. No one was in sight. Under a tree lay a rocking-chair, which had been tumbled over; and nearer the door lay a piece of needlework, which some one had dropped. These were Eric's signs, but the others would not believe in them.

Just as they passed, however, they heard the plaintive sound of a baby's sleepy cry.

"There, now! didn't I tell you?" said Eric, in triumph.

"But how did you know?" asked Katie.

"Why, don't you see, when he began to cry, his mother jumped up, and upset her chair, and dropped her work as she ran."

But now the long drive was over, and the children had found the last half of it shorter than the first after all.

MISS CARELESS

a wry' dis or'der   plunged   un com'fort a ble

PART I

Miss Careless was a good little girl who loved her papa and mamma dearly. But she had one bad fault. She took no care of anything.

Now her parents knew that she should learn order. So, to their sorrow, they often had to punish her.

If her bed was in disorder, she was forced to wear her nightcap all day. Every time she upset her inkstand, the end of her nose was inked. Whenever she left her handkerchief lying about the house, it was fastened on her back. A shoe was once hung there, which had been found astray on the stairs.

Careless had a brother Paul. He was away from home in a boarding-school. Sometimes he had a holiday at home and then how happy Careless was to play with him!

One holiday they had put everything out of place in the parlor and dining room. Miss Careless was told that she must not leave her room all the next morning.

The next morning the rising sun found her seated on her bed in tears. Her room was to be her prison till dinner. And what a room it was!

Her pretty new dress was in a corner, half on the floor and half on a chair. One of her boots was under the bed and the other against the door. Two gray silk gloves were on each end of the mantelpiece. Last of all her little black velvet hat was lying on its side on the top of the water pitcher with its great white plume falling into the basin.

"How unhappy I am!" cried Careless. "Oh, why won't they let me play with Paul?"

The fairy Order was at that moment making her way through the house. She opened

the door and came into the room. How she frowned at the disorder!

"Are you not ashamed?" she cried.

"Of what, madam?"

"Look around your room!"

" Well, what is the matter with it ? "

" What! don't you see the frightful disorder ? There is not a single garment in its
place."

" Oh! that doesn't matter. Paul says that
it makes no difference where we put our
things at night, so long as we find them in
the morning."

" So you think it makes no difference where
you put your things! " cried the angry fairy.
" Well, you shall see."

With these words she touched the child
with her wand. Behold! little Careless flew
into pieces in every direction. The head
went in search of the hat on the water pitcher.
The body plunged into the dress across the
chair. Each foot regained its boot, the one
under the bed and the other against the door.
The hands made their way into the gloves on
each end of the mantelpiece. It all happened
in an instant.

" Now," said the fairy, " I am going to send
Master Paul to put all this in order. You

shall see whether it makes no difference where you put things."

The fairy Order went down into the courtyard, where she found Paul.

"Go upstairs to your sister's room. She needs you."

PART II

Paul obeyed the fairy Order and went to find Miss Careless. He saw no one in the room.

"What is the matter? Where are you?" he cried.

"Here," groaned the head. "Come quickly to my help, dear Paul. I am very uncomfortable on this water pitcher."

"No, come here," howled the body. "I can't bear this torture; the corner of the chair goes right through me."

"Don't leave me under the bed," cried the right foot.

"I am here by the door," said the left foot.

"Don't forget us on the mantelpiece," shouted the hands.

Paul hastened to pick up the feet, hands,

and head. "Don't worry, sister," he said, "I will set you to rights. It will not take me long."

Paul's task was quickly over. Then he raised his sister on her feet and cried, "There you are!"

But scarcely had he looked at his work than he uttered a loud cry. The head was turned awry. One of the feet, in its boot, hung on the left arm. A poor little hand was in the place of one foot. How Careless staggered as she tried to walk on one hand and one foot!

"Oh! Paul, what have you done?" cried the poor little girl. She tried to wipe her eyes, but the toe of her boot caught in her hair.

Paul was thunderstruck at what he had done. He pulled with all his might at his sister's head, hoping to put it in the right place.

Alas! it was too firmly fixed. Then Paul, too, burst into tears and cried and sobbed with Careless.

Doctors were sent for, but they could do nothing. Everybody talked at once. Such an uproar as there was!

Suddenly the fairy Order appeared.

"Well," she said to Careless, "do you think now that it makes no difference where you put your things? I will forgive you this once, but you must never forget this terrible lesson."

The fairy then touched the little girl with her wand. Instantly head, body, feet, and hands found their right places.

After this Careless became most neat and careful. When she grew up, the fairy Order married her to a prince who wished to have his house kept in perfect order. The prince was more pleased with her neatness than with her beautiful face.

Careless had learned her lesson well.

— MACÉ.

THE FAIRIES

Co lumb'kill   crisp'y   Slieve' league

Up the airy mountain,
   Down the rushy glen,
We daren't go a-hunting
   For fear of little men;
Wee folk, good folk,
   Trooping all together;
Green jacket, red cap,
   And white owl's feather!

Down along the rocky shore
   Some make their home;
They live on crispy pancakes
   Of yellow tide foam;
Some in the reeds
   Of the black mountain lake,
With frogs for their watchdogs,
   All night awake.

High on the hilltop
   The old king sits;

He is now so old and gray,
   He's nigh lost his wits.
With a bridge of white mist
   Columbkill he crosses,
On his stately journeys
   From Slieveleague to Rosses;
Or going up with music
   On cold starry nights,
To sup with the queen
   Of the gay Northern Lights.

They stole little Bridget
   For seven years long;
When she came down again,
   Her friends were all gone.
They took her lightly back,
   Between the night and morrow;
They thought that she was fast asleep,
   But she was dead with sorrow.
They have kept her ever since
   Deep within the lakes,
On a bed of flag leaves,
   Watching till she wakes.

By the craggy hillside,
  Through the mosses bare,
They have planted thorn trees
  For pleasure here and there.
Is any man so daring
  As dig them up in spite?
He shall find their sharpest thorns
  In his bed at night.

Up the airy mountain,
  Down the rushy glen,
We daren't go a-hunting
  For fear of little men;
Wee folk, good folk,
  Trooping all together;
Green jacket, red cap,
  And white owl's feather!

—William Allingham.

"SO – SO"

pet' ti coat	quar' rel ing	ex act' ly
duf' fle	dis grace'	quilt' ed

PART I

"Be sure, my child," said the widow to her little daughter, "that you always do just as you are told."

"Very well, mother."

"Or at any rate do what will do just as

well," said the small house dog, as he lay blinking at the fire.

"You darling!" cried little Joan, and she sat down on the hearth and hugged him.

"What a dear, kind house dog you are!" She meant what she said, for it does feel nice to have the sharp edges of one's duty a little softened off for one.

He was no particular kind of dog, but he was very smooth to stroke, and had a nice way of blinking with his eyes. So he was called So-So; and a very nice soft name it is.

The widow was only a poor woman, but she managed by her work to get many little comforts for herself and child.

One day, as she was going out, she said to her little daughter, "I am going out for two hours. Shut the house door and bolt the big wooden bar, and be sure that you do not open it for any reason whatever till I return. If strangers come, So-So may bark, which he can do as well as a bigger dog. Then they will go away.

" With this summer's savings I have bought
a quilted petticoat for you and a duffle cloak
for myself. If I get the work I am going after
to-day, I shall buy enough wool to knit warm
stockings for us both. So be patient till I
return, and then we will have the plum cake
that is in the cupboard for tea."

" Thank you, mother."

" Good-by, my child. Be sure you do
just as I have told you," said the widow.

" Very well, mother."

Little Joan shut the house door, and fastened the big bolt. The kitchen looked
gloomy when she had done it.

" I wish mother had taken us all three with
her. She could have locked the house and
put the key in her big pocket," said little Joan,
as she got into the rocking-chair, to put her
doll asleep.

" Yes, it would have been just as well," So-
So replied.

By and by Joan grew tired of hushabying
the doll. She took the three-legged stool and

sat down in front of the clock to watch the hands. After a while she drew a deep sigh.

"There are sixty seconds in every minute, So-So," said she.

"So I have heard," said So-So.

"And sixty whole minutes in every hour, So-So."

"You don't say so!" growled So-So. He was snuffing in every corner of the kitchen, looking for something to eat. At last he stood snuffing under the house door.

"The air smells fresh," he said.

"It's a beautiful day, I know," said little Joan. "I wish mother had allowed us to sit on the doorstep. We could have taken care of the house."

"Just as well," said So-So.

Little Joan came to smell the air at the key-hole, and, as So-So had said, it smelt very fresh. Besides, one could see from the window how fine the evening was.

"It's not exactly what Mother told us to do," said Joan, "but I do believe" —

PART II

By and by little Joan unfastened the bar, and opened the door, and she and the doll and So-So went out and sat on the door-step.

"It does just as well, and better," said little Joan, "for if any one comes we can see him coming up the field path."

"Just so," said So-So, blinking in the sunshine.

Suddenly Joan jumped up.

"Oh!" cried she, "there's a bird, a big bird. Dear So-So, can you see him? I can't because of the sun. What a queer noise he makes. Crake! crake! Oh, I can see him now! He is not flying, he is running, and he has gone into the corn. I do wish I were in the corn, I would catch him and put him in a cage."

"I'll catch him," said So-So. He put up his tail, and started off.

"No, no," cried Joan. "You are not to

go. You must stay and take care of the house, and bark if any one comes."

"You could scream, and that would do just as well," replied So-So, with his tail still up.

"No, it wouldn't," cried little Joan.

"Yes, it would," said So-So.

Whilst they were quarreling, an old woman came up to the door. She had a brown face, and black hair, and a very old red cloak.

"Good evening, my little dear," said she. "Are you all at home this evening?"

"Only three of us," said Joan: "I, and my doll, and So-So. Mother has gone to the town on business, and we are taking care of the house, but So-So wants to go after the bird we saw run into the corn."

"Was it a pretty bird, my little dear?" asked the old woman.

"It was a very curious one," said Joan, "and I should like to go after it myself, but we can't leave the house."

"I have some distance to go this evening," said the old woman, "but I do not object to a few minutes' rest. I will sit on the doorstep to oblige you, while you run down to the corn-field."

"But can you bark if any one comes?" asked little Joan. "For if you can't, So-So must stay with you."

"I can call you and the dog if I see any one coming, and that will do just as well," said the woman.

"So it will," replied little Joan; and off she ran to the cornfield, where So-So had run before her. He was bounding and barking and springing among the wheat stalks.

They did not catch the bird, though they stayed longer than they had intended.

"I daresay mother has come home," said little Joan, as they went back up the field-path. "I hope she won't think we ought to have stayed in the house."

"It was well taken care of," said So-So, "and that must do just as well."

When they reached the house, the widow had not come home.

But the old woman had gone, and she had taken the quilted petticoat and the duffle cloak, and the plum cake from the top shelf away with her. No more was ever heard of any of them.

"For the future, my child," said the widow, "I hope you will always do just as you are told, whatever So-So may say."

"I will, mother," said Joan. But the house dog sat and blinked. He dared not speak; he was in disgrace.

I do not feel quite sure about So-So. Wild dogs often mend their ways, and the faithful sometimes fall; but when any one begins by being only So-So, he is very apt to be So-So to the end. So-Sos so seldom change.

But this one was *very* soft and nice, and he got no cake that tea time. On the whole, we shall hope that he lived to be a Good Dog ever after.

—JULIANA HORATIA EWING.

ROBIN REDBREAST

Good-by, good-by to summer!
  For summer's nearly done;
The garden smiling faintly,
  Cool breezes in the sun;
Our thrushes now are silent,
  Our swallows flown away, —
But Robin's here with coat of brown,
  And ruddy breast knot gay.
Robin, Robin Redbreast,
  O Robin dear!
Robin sings so sweetly
  In the falling of the year.

Bright yellow, red, and
orange,
The leaves come down in
hosts;
The trees are Indian
princes,
But soon they'll turn to
ghosts;
The scanty pears and
apples
Hang russet on the bough;
It's autumn, autumn, au-
tumn late,
'Twill soon be winter now.
Robin, Robin Redbreast,
O Robin dear!
Robin sings so sweetly
In the falling of the year.
What now will this poor
Robin do?
For pinching days are
near.

The fireside for the cricket,
  The wheat stack for the mouse,
When trembling night winds whistle
  And moan all round the house.
The frosty ways like iron,
  The branches plumed with snow, —
Alas! in winter dead and dark,
  Where can poor Robin go?
Robin, Robin Redbreast,
  O Robin dear!
And a crumb of bread for Robin
  His little heart to cheer!

— WILLIAM ALLINGHAM.

A HOLIDAY HUNT

hol'i day	in ter rupt'ed	de liv'er ers
pur suit'	sti'fling	cap tiv'i ty
slaugh'tered	de fy'ing	Au gus'tus
fag'ots	chal'lenge	Reg'i nald

"Robert, is that you?" said Mr. Howard, coming out of his room.

"Yes, father; I am blowing a blast with

my cow horn. We are going to have a hunt."

" I must beg," said his father, " that you will blow through no cow horns in this house."

" May I in the garden ? "

" As much as you please, provided I am not near to hear it ; but now go along, and do not make a noise," and he shut the door of his study.

Bob's blasts brought his brothers and sisters, and many cousins into the bargain, round him, for the house was full of cousins. All the cousins were come for three whole days, and these days were to be holidays.

"Let us see how many there are of us," said Bob. " Anna, Mary, Philip, Jane, Kate, Reginald, Carry, Bob, William, and Augustus. But where are Emma and Polly ? "

" In the nursery, counting their money boxes," cried Philip. " I'll fetch them ! "

" Emma and Polly make twelve ; Quiz makes the thirteenth."

Quiz was all the time whining and barking,

and jumping up and running to and fro in the desire to be off. Augustus Clifford proposed that six should be hounds and six deer. All wished to be hounds, so Bob proposed that they should draw lots.

Counting their Money Boxes.

"I will tear this letter in strips," said William, "and write our names upon them. Then we will draw. The first name is to be a deer, the next a hound, and so on."

Jane, Mary, Anna, and William were to be hounds; Emma, Kate, Polly, Reginald, and Philip were to be deer.

"Come, make haste," said William, "or we shall be drawing all day. The next is to hunt."

"Draw, Carry," said Bob.

"Robert and Quiz," said Caroline. "Let me see this time: Carry — I myself! I am determined I shall not be caught."

Bob drew the next slip.

"Who do you think is drawn now?" he said, looking at the paper. "Augustus."

"Am I to hunt or to be hunted?" asked Augustus.

"To hunt."

"I am certain to catch you, Carry," said Augustus.

"We'll see," said Caroline.

"You must give us," said Reginald, "a start of a quarter of an hour."

"By all means," said William. "A quarter of an hour is none too much."

Bob, who was always for giving more than was asked, said : —

"You shall have twenty minutes."

"That will do famously," said Carry.

"Has any one a watch amongst us?" asked Bob.

"Yes, I have," said Philip. "Take it," he said, flinging it to Robert.

The herd of deer stepped off at full speed till they came to five lanes. Here each deer separated and took a lane. Some scrambled up banks and made their way across the country, and Philip took the direction to Lidwell.

The cow horn sounds three several times: the twenty minutes are expired. Bob and his crew are in hot pursuit. How many a deer will be slaughtered to-day!

"Oh, me, I hear the horn!" said Caroline, leaning over a gate, "and I feel as though I shall be caught. Augustus will think of nothing but me."

"And I," answered Emma — "oh, where shall I go? I know I shall be caught."

"Emma, are you there in the lane?" said Caroline. "Come with me. Pray do let us share our fates together."

"Oh, yes, let us," said Emma. "I had rather run with you, for I am so frightened. If I am caught, I know I shall give a horrid scream!"

"I shall yell outright," said Carry, climbing over the gate and joining her cousin in the lane.

"Did you hear some voices below?" said Emma. "I am quite sure I heard Augustus and Bob."

"Yes, and Quiz," said Caroline. "Follow, follow me. If we can but gain the cow shed, we can hide there."

The two girls ran across three or four fields, and arrived panting at the shed. An old woodman stood before it.

"Hide us!" said Carry.

"Hide you, miss? What are you afraid of?"

"Oh, hide us, hide us, or we shall be caught!"

"Creep," · said the good-natured man,

" creep through that hole close to the rabbits, and I will cover it with fagots. They shan't find you out."

They both crept panting into the hole.

" Don't tell of us."

"Not I," said the man, laughing at the girls. He had only just time to cover them with fagots, when Bob and Augustus made their appearance.

"Here, here!" said Bob to the man, who was standing with a few fagots in his hand.

" Hard of hearing," said the man, pretending to be deaf.

"Have you seen two little girls?" screamed Bob into the old man's ear.

Carry chuckled.

" Hard of hearing," again answered the man.

" Very, indeed," said Bob. " Gussy, speak to him."

" Have you seen two —— "

" Dogs?" interrupted the man.

Carry and Emma trembled as they sat on the potato heap behind the fagots.

"He will tell them all," said Caroline in a whisper to Emma.

Quiz, while this conversation was going on, jumped up and tore at the fagots, barking most furiously.

"That horrid Quiz will betray us," whispered Emma.

"I am afraid so," said Caroline.

"Call your dog away," said the old man in a gruff voice, addressing himself to Quiz.

"Don't think that you will have my young rabbits."

"Dear old man!" said Carry. "I could hug him!"

"He means us by his young rabbits," said Emma in a whisper.

"Have you just found that out?" said Carry, stifling a laugh.

"Don't, don't laugh, pray," said Emma.

"If I get home," whispered Caroline, "he shall have the shilling."

"I will add sixpence," said Emma.

"Now, young masters, if your dog kills my rabbits, I'll knock him on the head."

"And I'll knock you," said Augustus, in great wrath.

"Hush!" said Bob. "How can you speak so to an old man?"

"Well, but I do not think he heard me," said Augustus. "He is so deaf."

"He did, though, Master Gussy," whispered Caroline, stuffing her hand into her mouth to prevent laughing.

"I am sure I saw them go this way," said Bob.

"So did I," said Augustus; "they are hard by, depend upon it."

Carry gave a start, and down fell a piece of wood. But the boys did not notice it.

"I would give something to have a hunt for those white rabbits," said Augustus.

"Now, I think I know where they are," said Bob. "They're in the log house in the wood yonder. Carry dearly loves to hide there, because it is so difficult to climb."

The two girls, trembling with hope, put both their hands into their mouths to prevent laughing.

"Come along," said Bob, "and we'll look for them there."

Quiz was not to be made a fool of. He did not choose to follow his young master down the hill, as he knew the deer were in the hut. There he stood, tearing at the fagots, and howling and barking.

The man lifted his stick, as if to strike the

dog, and Bob, laughing, said, "Catch him, and I will give you leave to strike him."

"Well, then," said the old man, "carry him away with you, for I am afraid for my young rabbits."

"Really, he is a dear old man," thought Carry.

Robert and Augustus did not hear what he said, for they were on their way to the log house. The old man opened the door of a tool house belonging to the shed, and Quiz had the folly to run into it. Thereupon the man popped to the door, and left Quiz to howl and almost choke with rage.

When Bob and Gussy were at some distance, the old man removed the fagots and said, "Make haste, my little rabbits, and away home with you."

"Thank you! thank you a thousand times!" said they both.

"Away, away with you, my little ladies!" said he. "When shall I let out the dog? It's a nice dog, sure."

"In about two minutes," said Carry, "or, rather, now. We have caught him; he has not caught us. I will open the door."

She did so, and Quiz, jumping up, licked Carry's face for this kindness, and thought, "I won't catch Emma and you." Then he danced round them and ran off in pursuit of his master.

Caroline and Emma stood upon a hillock at a little distance from the shed, and shouted out, "Bobby! Gussy! Gussy! Bobby!"

The boys, who heard the sounds, turned round and beheld them. "Look, look!" said Bob; "there they are above us, defying us."

"They were behind the fagots all the time, I will answer for it," said Augustus.

Caroline and Emma threw down their gloves as a challenge to hunt them. Augustus set off after them.

"After them, Quiz!" said Bob.

But Quiz had too much honor to pursue his deliverers from captivity. He turned round, whining softly, as if he meant to say, "I shall

117

do no such thing.   She opened the door of the
log house for me."

"Well, you know best," said Bob, laughing
at Quiz; "but we will away to the log house
together.   There may be some sport there.
Gussy won't be able to catch them, they are
so far before him."

Were I to tell you all the adventures of this
hunt, my story would never come to an end.
It is enough to know they all returned in
safety, and no fox hunters on the finest
horses ever enjoyed a hunt more.

THE OWL AND THE PUSSY-CAT

gui tar'   run'ci ble   tar'ried

The Owl and the Pussy-Cat went to sea
  In a beautiful pea-green boat;
They took some honey, and plenty of money
  Wrapped up in a five-pound note.

The Owl looked up to the moon above,
  And sang to a small guitar,

"O lovely Pussy! O Pussy, my love,
What a beautiful Pussy you are, —
You are,
What a beautiful Pussy you are!"

Pussy said to the Owl, "You elegant fowl!
How wonderful sweet you sing!
Oh, let us be married, — too long we have tar-
ried, —
But what shall we do for a ring?"

They sailed away for a year and a day
  To the land where the Bong tree grows,
And there in the wood, a piggy-wig stood
  With a ring in the end of his nose, —
        His nose,
  With a ring in the end of his nose.

"Dear Pig, are you willing to sell for one
    shilling
  Your ring?" Said the piggy, "I will."
So they took it away, and were married next
    day
  By the turkey who lives on the hill.

They dined upon mince and slices of quince,
  Which they ate with a runcible spoon.
And hand in hand on the edge of the sand
  They danced by the light of the moon, —
        The moon,
  They danced by the light of the moon.

EDWARD LEAR.

CHRISTMAS BELLS

Wake me to-night, my mother dear,
That I may hear
The Christmas Bells, so soft and clear,
To high and low glad tidings tell
How God the Father loved us well.

—JOHN KEBLE.

OLD CHRISTMAS

carle   a nigh'   an'cient

Now he who knows old Christmas,
  He knows a carle of worth;
For he is as good a fellow
  As any upon the earth.

He comes warm cloaked and coated,
  And buttoned up to the chin,
And soon as he comes anigh the door
  We open and let him in.

We know that he will not fail us,
  So we sweep the hearth up clean;
We set him in the old armchair,
  And a cushion whereon to lean.

And with sprigs of holly and ivy
  We make the house look gay,

Just out of old regard to him,
   For it was his ancient way.

He must be a rich old fellow :
   What money he gives away!
There is not a lord in England
   Could equal him any day.

Good luck unto old Christmas,
   And long life, let us sing,
For he doth more good unto the poor
   Than many a crownèd king!

                 — MARY HOWITT.

THE TINY MAHOGANY BOX

A CHRISTMAS STORY

ma hog'a ny   o be'di ence   Sar a to'ga

Dear, bright-eyed, laughing children, I am going to tell you a true Christmas story.

Once upon a time there were two little children named Elsie and Pearl. They lived in a small white house in the country, and a very nice little house it was, too. In the summer time gay morning-glories and honey-suckles crept all over the windows, so that they didn't need a bit of a curtain. You would have liked that, wouldn't you?

The mother of Elsie and Pearl was a poor widow who owned nothing in the world but the cottage, a cow, and some chickens. She earned her living by selling milk and eggs to the

rich people who came to spend the summer time in the country.

But this year the rich people did not come. They went to Saratoga instead. Christmas

Eve found the poor woman without any money. She could not buy a Christmas dinner; she could not buy presents for Elsie and Pearl. Wasn't that *too* bad! Not a penny on Christmas Eve, of *all* times in the year!

The children had gone to bed, and the poor mother sat alone in the room that served for both parlor and kitchen. Would you like to know how this room looked? I will tell you.

On the floor was a warm rag carpet made by the widow and Elsie and Pearl. Around the room stood four wooden chairs and a wooden table, scrubbed as white as new milk. The mantelshelf was very high, and on it stood two candlesticks, a clock, and a tiny mahogany box. A wood fire was blazing on the hearth, and Elsie's and Pearl's stockings were hanging one on each andiron.

They had gone to bed believing that Santa Claus would bring them some presents. While the mother was grieving because she could not go to the new store in the village to buy them pretty gifts, they were smiling in their sleep. They were dreaming of handfuls of sugarplums and all sorts of beautiful toys.

"Ah!" thought the widow, "how well I remember, when I was a little girl, running to my stocking early Christmas morning. Oh, my dear mother, how kind she was! And to think that I love Elsie and Pearl just as she loved me, and yet I can buy them nothing. I declare I could cry."

And she *did* cry, throwing her checked apron over her head and leaning back in her rocking-chair. Just then the clock struck seven, and the tired woman fell fast asleep.

She had a beautiful dream. The room was suddenly lighted with a great light, and her dear mother stood before her. Her dress was white as a snowflake, and the old sweet smile was on her lips.

She took her daughter's hand and said, very gently, "Child, you forget that God is watching over you. Do you remember the little box that I put into your stocking many years ago? It was locked, and I told you never to open it unless you became *very, very* poor. You have kept your promise so faithfully that you have never even thought of opening it. I have come to tell you that you may unlock the box. But never again lose faith in your Father above."

The widow awoke, but she remembered all that her mother had said. She took down the tiny box, placed it on the table, and began looking for the key. At last it tumbled out of an old black silk bag that she found in a trunk.

She quickly unlocked the box, *and what do you think she saw?*

A whole row of gold pieces, lying on a soft bed of cotton! For a moment the widow could not move, she was so amazed. Then she fell upon her knees and thanked God.

Quickly she put on her thick hood and cloak and started for the village store. When she returned she had her arms full and a bundle tied on her back.

Oh, what a happy little house that was on Christmas morning! Elsie and Pearl were running round at daybreak to see what Santa Claus had brought them.

Each stocking was filled so full with sugar-plums, cakes, oranges, that it looked as though it would burst.

Two of the chairs were placed close together. On the back of one hung a new cloak for Elsie, and on the back of the other a new cloak for Pearl. On the seat of one lay a new pair of shoes and a new crimson dress for Elsie, and on the other, new shoes and a crimson dress for Pearl.

And that was not all. On the white wooden table lay a plump turkey, some nice large potatoes, and a plum pudding. And the market basket! The cover couldn't fit on because the basket was so crowded with parcels of raisins, tea, flour, and everything good to eat.

So you see, dear children, how the widow was rewarded for her obedience. Had she broken her promise, the money would all have been spent. She would have had no Christmas dinner, and Elsie and Pearl no Christmas presents.

— MARGARET EYTINGE.

THE STORY OF WILLIAM TELL

| ty'rant | op press'ing | Gess'ler |
| Aus'tri a | Switz'er land | fu'ri ous |

Across the sea is the small country of Switzerland. Though small, Switzerland is very beautiful. It has lofty mountains, green valleys, and lakes as blue as the sky.

The Swiss love their country dearly. They are proud of her, too, because they have made and kept her free.

But over six hundred years ago Switzerland was not free. The country of Austria was oppressing Switzerland greatly. Proud and cruel Austrians were to be found in the Swiss cities.

These Austrians ruled the people harshly. One of these rulers was named Gessler.

Gessler wanted to test the people to see who were friends of Austria and who were not. He hung the Austrian emperor's hat on a tall pole in the market-place. Then he ordered every one who passed to bow down before it.

Imagine the feelings of the free Swiss! Many of them, however, bowed through fear.

But there was one brave man who would not bow. His name was William Tell. He glanced carelessly at the hat and then passed on.

The tyrant Gessler was furious. He ordered that Tell should be brought before him.

Now Tell was an archer of great skill. As soon as he saw Tell, Gessler cried: "Bold man, I will punish you well. You must shoot an apple from the head of your son. Aim well, for if you fail, my soldiers shall kill your son before your eyes."

They brought Tell's son, a little fellow of seven years. They bound him against a tree

and set an apple on his flaxen head. The
little boy smiled at his father; he did not
tremble. All the people held their breath.

Tell raised his bow, then dropped it.
His hand shook with fear.

"Shoot, father," cried the little lad; "you
will not miss."

Instantly Tell let go his bowstring.

Straight flew the arrow. The two halves
of the apple fell to the ground. The boy
was safe.

As Tell stooped to hug his child, a
second arrow fell from his coat. Now Gessler had told him that he could have but
one arrow.

"Man," cried Gessler, "why have you
this arrow?"

"To shoot thee, tyrant, had I slain my son."

—Fanny E. Coe.

A DONKEY RACE[1]

com mo'tion   hob'bled   in tel'li gent

[The donkey who tells the story has had many adventures.
His last mistress was a little sick child who finally died.
Thereupon her parents turned the donkey adrift.]

All the next winter I had no one to take
care of me. I had to live in the forest, where
I found scarcely enough to keep me from
dying of hunger and thirst.

When the spring came, I went one day to

[1] Copyright, 1901, by D. C. Heath and Company. Used by permission.

a village on the edge of the forest. I was surprised to find quite a commotion there.

The people were walking up and down; everybody had on his Sunday clothes; and, what was stranger still, all the donkeys in the neighborhood seemed to be there. They were sleek and fat, their heads were decorated with flowers and leaves, and not one of them was in harness or had a rider.

I trotted up to see if I could find out what all this was about. Suddenly one of the boys who was standing there saw me, and shouted, "Oh, I say, look here! here's a fine donkey!"

"My word!" said another, "how well groomed he is! and how fat and well fed!" and they roared with laughter.

"I suppose he's come to run in the donkey race," said a third, "but *he* won't win the prize! No fear!"

I was very much annoyed at these rude jokes and personal remarks, but I thought I should enjoy taking part in the race, so I listened again.

"Where are they going to run?" asked an old dame who had just come up.

"In the meadow by the mill," said a man named Andrew.

"How many donkeys are there?" asked the old woman.

"Sixteen, Mother Evans, and the one that comes in first will win a silver watch and a bag of money."

"Oh, deary me!" said Mother Evans, "I do wish *I* had a donkey. I *should* so like to have a watch. I've never had the money to buy one."

I liked the look of the old woman; I was justly proud of my running; I had been so long in the forest that I was not too fat, as some of the prize donkeys were; and so I *would* take part in the race. I trotted up to the others, and took my place among them, and then, to attract attention, I opened my mouth and brayed vigorously.

"Oh, you stop that!" cried out a man named Bill. "Hi! you there, donkey, you just stop that music, will you? and get out of there! *You* can't run, you shabby brute! and, besides, you don't belong to anybody."

I held my tongue, but I didn't budge an inch. Some laughed, and others were getting angry, when old Mother Evans said: —

" Well, he can have *me* for his mistress. I take him into my service from this minute. So now he can run for me."

" Well," said Bill, " do as you like, mother. Only, if you want him to run, you've got to put a quarter into the bag the Squire has yonder."

" All right, my dear," said Mother Evans. She hobbled off to where the Squire was sitting, and paid her subscription into the bag.

" Very good," said the Squire; " put Mrs. Evans's name down, Richard."

So the clerk put down my new mistress's name. We were all drawn up in a line in the meadow. The Squire said, " One, two, three, and away!" The boys who held the donkeys let them go, and away we galloped as hard as we could, while the crowd ran cheering alongside.

The sixteen donkeys had not gone a hundred yards before I was in front of them all, an easy first. I thought I *would* beat them all now, at any rate, and I flew along as if I had wings. I passed proudly before the winning post, not only first, but a long way ahead of all the rest, amid loud cheers from those who had no donkeys in the race.

The Squire sat at a table to give away the prizes. Mother Evans, who was almost be-

side herself with delight, stroked and patted
me, and led me up to the table with her to
receive the first prize.

"Here, my good woman," said the Squire;
and he was going to hand the watch and the
bag of money to the old woman.

"Please, your worship, it isn't fair!" cried
Bill and Andrew. "That donkey doesn't
really belong to Mother Evans any more
than it does to us! *Our* donkeys really
got in first, not counting this one. The
watch and money ought to be ours. It isn't
fair!"

"Did Mrs. Evans pay her quarter into the
bag?" said the Squire.

"Well, your worship, she did—"

"Did any of you object to her doing so at
the time?" asked the Squire.

"Well, no, your worship, but—"

"Did you raise any objections when the
donkeys were just going to start?"

"Well, no, sir, but—"

"Very well, then. It's all perfectly fair,

and Mrs. Evans gets the watch and bag of
money."

"Please, sir, it isn't fair, it isn't fair!
You —"

When I heard this, I at once put my head
down on the table, and taking up the watch
and bag in my teeth, put them into Mother
Evans's hands. This intelligent action on my
part made the people roar with laughter, and
won for me thunders of applause.

"There!" said the Squire, "the donkey
has decided in favor of Mother Evans; and,"
he added, with a smile, looking at Bill and
Andrew, "I don't think *he* is the biggest
donkey present!"

"Bravo, your worship!" "Good for you!"
resounded on all sides. And every one began
to laugh at Andrew and Bill, who went away
looking cross and ill-tempered.

And was *I* pleased? No, not at all. My
pride was hurt. The Squire had been very
rude to me. It was too much.

I declined to stay in a place where I was so

insulted, and I turned tail and trotted away from such an ignorant set of people.

—Madame de Segur.

THE TREE

trem'bled leaf'lets quiv'er ing

The Tree's early leaf buds were bursting their
 brown ;
" Shall I take them away ? " said the Frost,
 sweeping down.
  " No, leave them alone
  Till the blossoms have grown,"
Prayed the Tree, while he trembled from root-
 let to crown.

The Tree bore his blossoms, and all the birds
 sung :
" Shall I take them away ? " said the Wind,
 as he swung.
  " No, leave them alone
  Till the berries have grown,"
Said the Tree, while his leaflets quivering hung.

The Tree bore his fruit in the midsummer
    glow:
Said the girl, "May I gather thy berries
    now ? "
      " Yes, all thou canst see :
      Take them ; all are for thee,"
Said the Tree, while he bent down his laden
    boughs low.
            —BJÖRNSTJERNE BJÖRNSON.

LITTLE SAMUEL

min'is tered	E'li	in iq'ui ty
per ceived'	eph'od	Is'ra el
proph'et	es tab'lished	sac'ri fice
re strained'	Be er she'ba	Sam'u el

But Samuel ministered before the Lord,
being a child, girded with a linen ephod.

Moreover, his mother made him a little
coat, and brought it to him from year to
year, when she came up to offer the yearly
sacrifice.

And the child Samuel ministered unto the

Lord before Eli. And the word of the Lord was precious in those days; there was no open vision.

And it came to pass at that time, when Eli was laid down in his place, and his eyes

 began to wax dim, that he could not see;

And ere the lamp of God went out in the temple of the Lord, where the ark of God was, and Samuel was laid down to sleep;

That the Lord called Samuel: and he answered, Here am I.

And he ran unto Eli, and said, Here am I; for thou calledst me. And he said, I called not; lie down again. And he went and lay down.

And the Lord called yet again, Samuel. And Samuel arose and went to Eli, and said, Here am I; for thou didst call me. And he answered, I called not, my son; lie down again.

Now Samuel did not yet know the Lord, neither was the word of the Lord yet revealed unto him.

And the Lord called Samuel again the third time. And he arose and went to Eli, and said, Here am I; for thou didst call me. And Eli perceived that the Lord called the child.

Therefore Eli said unto Samuel, Go, lie down: and it shall be, if he call thee, that thou shalt say, Speak, Lord; for thy servant heareth. So Samuel went and lay down in his place.

And the Lord came, and stood, and called as at other times, Samuel, Samuel. Then Samuel answered, Speak; for thy servant heareth.

And the Lord said to Samuel, Behold, I will do a thing in Israel, at which both the ears of every one that heareth it shall tingle.

In that day I will perform against Eli all things which I have spoken concerning his house: when I begin I will also make an end.

For I have told him that I will judge his house .for ever for the iniquity which he knoweth; because his sons made themselves vile, and he restrained them not.

And Samuel lay until the morning and opened the doors of the house of the Lord. And Samuel feared to show Eli the vision.

Then Eli called Samuel, and said, Samuel, my son. And he answered, Here am I.

And he said, What is the thing that the Lord hath said unto thee? I pray thee hide it not from me: God do so to thee, and more also, if thou hide anything from me of all things that he said unto thee.

And Samuel told him every whit, and hid nothing from him. And he said, It is the Lord: let him do what seemeth him good.

And Samuel grew, and the Lord was with him, and did let none of his words fall to the ground.

And all Israel, from Dan even to Beer-
sheba, knew that Samuel was established to
be a prophet of the Lord.   —The Bible.

IN FEBRUARY

The birds have been singing to-day,
  And saying, " The spring is near!
The sun is as warm as in May,
  And the deep-blue heavens are clear."

The little bird on the boughs
  Of the somber snow-laden pine
Thinks : " Where shall I build me a house,
  And how shall I make it fine ?

" For the season of snow is past;
  The mild south wind is on high;
And the scent of the spring is cast
  From his wing as he hurries by."

The little birds twitter and cheep
  To their loves on the leafless larch;
But seven foot deep the snow-wreaths sleep,
  And the year hath not worn to March.
            —John Addington Symonds.

BRUCE AND THE SPIDER

toiled   fail'ure   dis heart'ened

There was once a king of Scotland whose name was Robert Bruce. He had need to be both brave and wise, for the times in which he lived were wild and rude. The king of England was at war with him, and had led a great army into Scotland to drive him out of the land.

Battle after battle had been fought. Six times had Bruce led his brave little army against his foes; and six times had his men been beaten and driven into flight. At last his army was scattered, and he was forced to hide himself in the woods and in lonely places among the mountains.

One rainy day, Bruce lay on the ground under a rude shed, listening to the patter of the raindrops on the roof above him. He was tired and sick at heart, and ready to give up all hope. It seemed to him that there was no use to try to do anything more.

As he lay thinking, he saw a spider over his head, making ready to weave her web. He watched her as she toiled slowly and with great care. Six times she tried to throw her frail thread from one beam to another, and six times it fell short.

"Poor thing!" said Bruce. "You, too, know what it is to fail."

But the spider did not lose hope with the sixth failure. With still more care she made ready to try the seventh time. Bruce almost forgot his own troubles as he watched her swing herself out upon the slender line. Would she fail again? No! The thread was carried safely to the beam and fastened there.

"I, too, will try a seventh time!" cried Bruce.

He arose and called his men together. He told them of his plans, and sent them out with messages of cheer to his disheartened people. Soon there was an army of brave Scotchmen around him. Another battle was fought, and the king of England was glad to go back into his own country.

I have heard it said that, after that day, no one by the name of Bruce would ever hurt a spider. The lesson which the little creature had taught the king was never forgotten.

—JAMES BALDWIN.

BRUCE AND THE BLOODHOUND

com'rades   col lect'ed   Gal'lo way

Many people of the Galloway were unfriendly to Bruce. They had heard that he was in their country with only sixty men. They collected two hundred men and brought with them two or three bloodhounds.

These hounds could chase a man by the
scent of his footsteps, as foxhounds chase a
fox. Although the dog does not see the

person whose trace he is put upon, he follows
him over every step of the way.

Good King Robert knew of their plans.
So he placed his men near a deep river, which
was crossed by but one ford. The ford was
so narrow that only two men could cross side
by side.

Bruce left his men to sleep a half mile from the river. He himself, with two of his soldiers, guarded the ford.

They heard a dog barking in the distance. "It may be only a shepherd's dog," thought Bruce; "I will not waken my tired men for that."

Time passed, and the cry of the hound drew nearer. Soon Bruce began to hear the noise of the horses and the ringing of armor. He said to himself, "The enemy comes!"

King Robert thought, "If I go to alarm my friends, these Galloway men will cross the ford easily. That would be a pity. This is such a fine place for a fight!"

So he sent the two men to awaken their comrades, while he stayed alone by the ford. Very soon he saw by the bright light of the moon that the other shore was full of men and horses. How the dogs barked when they saw the king standing by the bank!

The leaders plunged into the river. What was one man against so many?

But alas for them! they could only pass the ford one by one. Bruce killed the first man with his long spear. His wounded horse fell on the narrow path, and so blocked this end of the ford.

Bruce killed five or six more of his enemies. Others were drowned in the river. The rest were frightened and drew back.

Then they cried, "See! it is but one man. Our honor demands his death!" They sprang forward again with fierce shouts.

Just then the king's soldiers came up to the ford. The Galloway men saw them and gave up the fight.

— *Adapted from* SIR WALTER SCOTT.

ANOTHER BLOODHOUND STORY

| kins'man | Co'myn | hes'i tate |
| sep'a ra ted | fu'gi tive | sin'gled |

King Robert once owned a fine blood-hound. The dog loved him dearly and would follow him everywhere. After a time the dog came to belong to the Earl of Lorn.

Now the earl hated King Robert. This was because the king had once killed the earl's kinsman, the Red Comyn.

John of Lorn said to himself, "Now that the king is a fugitive, I will track him down with his own hound. Then I will kill him!"

The hound quickly got the scent. A great company of Bruce's enemies followed.

Bruce knew they were coming, and he divided his forces into three parts. When the hound reached the place where the men had separated, he did not hesitate. He immediately followed the party led by Bruce.

Bruce then divided his party again. He sent the men in all directions, hoping the hound would lose the scent. He had only one man with him, his foster brother.

But the hound did not once hesitate. He singled out the path of Bruce and followed hard on the track.

John of Lorn now sent five men to kill Bruce and his foster brother.

When they saw the five men coming,

Bruce said to his brother, "Will you fight for me?" "To the last drop of my blood," he replied.

So they turned against the five so bravely that they slew them all. Then they hastened away.

Presently they came to a stream. "Huzza!" cried King Robert, "now at last we may baffle that wretched hound!"

They waded out into the stream and walked in the water for a long distance. At last they landed many hundred yards down the stream.

When the men of Lorn came to the river, the hound was puzzled for the first time. He ran up and down the shore, trying to find the track. It was in vain.

Thanks to the little river, the wicked plans of Lorn had failed. Bruce was saved once more!

—Fanny E. Coe.

HOW A FARMER TOOK A CASTLE

| de fend'ed | port cul'lis | Lith'gow |
| Bin'nock | sta'tioned | gov' ern or |

Once upon a time there lived a farmer named Binnock. He loved King Robert and Scotland. He wished he could do something to help their cause.

Near his home was the strong castle of Lithgow. This castle was held by the English. Binnock resolved to gain it for his king.

The castle was near a lake and was defended by gates and a portcullis. A portcullis is a sort of door made of iron cross pieces like a grate. It has not hinges like a door, but is drawn up by pulleys and let down when any danger approaches. It may be dropped in a moment, and, as it has great iron spikes at the bottom, it crushes all that it falls upon.

It was one of Binnock's duties to supply the castle with hay. The English governor had just ordered several cart loads.

"Armed men sprang from the cart."

(158)

Binnock loaded his wagon with hay. In the wagon, covered by the hay, he placed eight strong men. Each was well armed.

He stationed a party of his friends near the castle gate. When he gave the signal they were to come to his help. The chosen signal was, "Call all, call all!"

In the morning Binnock set out to deliver the hay. The cart was driven by Binnock's servant, a strong, brave man who carried a sharp hatchet. The farmer himself walked beside the cart.

The castle watchman knew that the hay was expected. Seeing only two men, he opened the gate and raised the portcullis.

When the cart came under the gateway, the driver cut the horses loose. The horses went ahead, leaving the cart under the gate. Just then Binnock shouted, "Call all, call all!" The armed men sprang from the cart and those near the gate rushed against the English guard.

The Englishmen tried to shut the gates, but

the cart was in the way. They dropped the portcullis, but it caught in the cart and did not reach the ground.

So the Scottish men entered the fortress and killed the English or took them prisoners.

In this way Farmer Binnock won Lithgow Castle for his king.

— Adapted from SIR WALTER SCOTT.

THE BLACK DOUGLAS

nick'named   un a wares'   Doug'las

In Scotland, in the time of King Robert Bruce, there lived a brave man whose name was Douglas. His hair and beard were black and long, and his face was tanned and dark; and for this reason people nicknamed him the Black Douglas. He was a good friend of the king, and one of his strongest helpers.

In the war with the English, who were trying to drive Bruce from Scotland, the Black Douglas did many brave deeds; and the English people became very much afraid of him. By and by the fear of him spread all through the land. Nothing could frighten an English lad more than to tell him that the Black Douglas was not far away. Women told their children, when they were naughty, that the Black Douglas would get them ; and this made them very quiet and good.

There was a large castle in Scotland which the English had taken early in the war. The Scottish soldiers wanted very much to take it again, and the Black Douglas and his men went one day to see what they could do. It happened to be a holiday, and most of the English soldiers in the castle were eating, and drinking, and having a merry time. But they had left watchmen on the wall to see that the Scottish soldiers did not come upon them una-wares ; and so they felt quite safe.

In the evening, when it was growing dark, the wife of one of the soldiers went up on the wall with her child in her arms. As she looked over into the fields below the castle, she saw some dark objects moving toward the foot of the wall. In the dusk she could not make out what they were, and so she pointed them out to one of the watchmen.

"Pooh, pooh!" said the watchman. "Those are nothing to frighten us. They are the farmer's cattle, trying to find their way home. The farmer himself is enjoying the holiday, and has forgotten to bring them in. If the Douglas should happen this way before morning, he will be sorry for his carelessness."

But the dark objects were not cattle. They were the Black Douglas and his men, creeping on hands and feet toward the foot of the castle wall. Some of them were dragging ladders behind them through the grass. They would soon be climbing to the top of the wall. None of the English soldiers dreamed that they were within many miles of the place.

The woman watched them until the last one had passed around a corner out of sight. She was not afraid, for in the darkening twilight they looked indeed like cattle. After a while she began to sing to her child : —

"Don't be so sure about that!"

"Hush ye, hush ye, little pet ye,
   Hush ye, hush ye, do not fret ye,
   The Black Douglas shall not get ye."

All at once a gruff voice was heard behind her, saying, "Don't be so sure about that!"

She looked around, and there stood Black Douglas himself. At the same time a Scottish soldier climbed up a ladder and leaped upon the wall; and then there came another and another and another, until the wall was covered with them. Soon there was hot fighting in every part of the castle. But the English were so taken by surprise that they could not do much. Many of them were killed, and in a little while the Black Douglas and his men were the masters of the castle which by right belonged to them.

As for the woman and her child, the Black Douglas would not suffer any one to harm them. After a while they went back to England; and whether the mother made up any more songs about the Black Douglas, I cannot tell.

— JAMES BALDWIN.

THE HEART OF BRUCE

liege	out num'bered	stead
Pal'es tine	stir'rups	Span'iards
Sar'a cens	Mel'rose	prec'ious

After many years King Robert lay dying. He said to those about him, " I would speak with Douglas."

The good Lord Douglas came to the bedside. " Douglas, I am dying," said the king. And Douglas bowed his head; for he knew that the king spoke the truth.

" One evil deed I remember now with sorrow. The death of the Red Comyn rests heavy on my soul. I had always hoped that sometime I could fight for our Lord in Palestine, and so win my pardon. But I shall never see the Holy Land.

" When I am gone, take my heart with thee and go in my stead. That will show all men what I would have done. Wilt thou go, old friend ? "

And Douglas said, " I promise, my King."

Then King Robert was content, for he knew that Douglas was as true as steel.

After Bruce's death, Lord Douglas made ready for his journey to the Holy Land. The heart of Bruce was placed in a silver case which Douglas wore about his neck on a silver chain. Many brave knights joined Douglas.

They set sail and left far behind their dear country of Scotland. Halfway on their journey they stopped in Spain. The king of Spain welcomed them gladly.

"Why do you go so far as the Holy Land?" he said. "Here are many Saracens."

It was the Saracens whom Bruce had wished to fight in the Holy Land.

Douglas said to his men, "The enemies of Our Lord and of King Robert are here in Spain. Shall we not stay and help this good king in the battle to-morrow?" His men agreed.

On the morrow a great battle was fought between the Saracens on one side, and the

Spaniards and the Scottish knights on the other. The Saracens at last gave way, and the Scottish knights galloped after them. They left the Spaniards far behind.

Soon Douglas and his men found themselves in great danger. The Saracens had returned, and now hemmed them in on all sides. The Scotsmen fought bravely, but the Saracens greatly outnumbered them.

Douglas understood their peril. He rose  in his stirrups, took the heart of Bruce, and hurled it into the ranks of the enemy, crying, " Pass first, my Liege, as thou were wont, and Douglas will follow thee or die."

Afterwards they found him dead upon the battlefield. Beneath him lay the heart of Bruce. He had fought his way to it and protected it even in death.

They carried back to Scotland the body
of the Douglas and the precious heart of
Bruce, which was buried in Melrose Abbey.

— FANNY E. COE.

WISHING

Ring-ting! I wish I were a primrose,
A bright yellow primrose, blowing in the
  spring!
  The stooping boughs above me,
  The wandering bee to love me,
The fern and moss to creep across,
  And the elm tree for our king!

Nay — stay! I wish I were an elm tree,
A great, lofty elm tree, with green leaves gay!
  The winds would set them dancing,
  The sun and moonshine glance in,
The birds would house among the boughs,
  And sweetly sing.

O — no! I wish I were a robin,
A robin or a little wren, everywhere to go;

Through forest, field, or garden,
And ask no leave or pardon,
Till winter comes with icy thumbs
To ruffle up our wing!

Well — tell! Where should I fly to,
Where go to sleep in the dark wood or dell?
Before a day was over,
Home comes the rover,
For mother's kiss — sweeter this
Than any other thing.

— WILLIAM ALLINGHAM.

THE FISHERMAN AND HIS WIFE

im prove'ment   mag nif'i cent   veg'e ta bles
en chant'ed   scep'ter   fu'ri ous ly

PART I

Once there was a fisherman and his wife
who lived together in a hovel by the seashore. The fisherman went out every day to
catch fish.

One day he drew up a great flounder.

The flounder said to him, " Fisherman, listen to me. Let me go. I am not a real fish, but an enchanted prince. So put me back into the water and let me swim away."

"Very well," said the fisher- man. He put him back into the clear water and got up and went home to his wife.

" Well, husband," said the wife, " have you caught nothing to-day ? "

" No," said the man, — " that is, I did catch a flounder, but as he said he was an enchanted prince, I let him go again."

" Then did you wish for nothing ? " said the wife.

" No," said the man; " what should I wish for ? "

"Oh dear!" said the wife, "it is so dreadful always to live in this wretched hovel. You might have wished for a little cottage. Go again and call him. I daresay he will give it to us."

When he went back, the sea was green and yellow, and not nearly so clear. He stood and said : —

> "Flounder, flounder, in the sea,
> Quickly, quickly come to me,
> For my wife, dame Isabel,
> Wishes what I dare not tell."

Then the flounder came swimming up.

"Well, what does she wish?"

"Oh," said the fisherman, "my wife says I ought to have wished for something. She does not wish to live any longer in the hovel. She would rather have a cottage."

"Home with you!" said the flounder; "she has it already."

So the man went home and found, instead of the hovel, a little cottage. His wife took him by the hand and said, "Come in and see if this is not a great improvement."

So they went in, and there was a beautiful little bedroom, a kitchen and larder, with iron and brass ware of the very best. At the back was a little yard with fowls and ducks, and a little garden full of green vegetables and fruit.

"Look," said the wife; "is not that nice?"

"Yes," said the man, "if this can only last, we shall be very well contented."

All went well for a fortnight. Then the wife said, "Look here, husband; the cottage is really too small. I think the flounder should get us a larger house. I should like to live in a large stone castle."

"Oh, my dear wife, the cottage is good enough. Why should we have a castle?"

"We want one," said the wife. "Go along with you. The flounder can give us one."

The man felt very unwilling; nevertheless he went.

When he came to the seaside, the water was purple, and dark blue, and gray, and thick. He stood and said: —

> " Flounder, flounder, in the sea,
> Quickly, quickly come to me,
> For my wife, dame Isabel,
> Wishes what I dare not tell."

"Well, what does she wish?" asked the flounder.

"Oh," said the man, "she wants to live in a large stone castle."

"Home with you! She is already standing before the door."

When the man reached home, in place of the cottage there stood a great castle of stone. His wife took him by the hand and said, "Let us enter."

In the castle was a broad hall with a marble pavement, and there were a great many servants, who led them through magnificent rooms. At the back of the castle was a fine large garden with the most beautiful flowers and fruit trees. There was also a park a mile long, with deer and oxen and sheep.

"There!" said the wife; "is not this beautiful?"

"Oh, yes," said the man; "if it will only last, we can live in this fine castle and be very well contented."

The next morning the wife looked out and saw the beautiful country lying all around.

"Husband, just look out of this window. Just think if we could only be king over all this country. Go to your fish and tell him we should like to be king."

"Now, wife, what should we be king for? I don't want to be king."

"Well," said the wife, "if you don't want to be king, I will be king. So go and do as I say, all the same."

The man went, feeling very much put out with his wife's folly.

PART II

When the fisherman came to the sea, the water was dark gray, and it was rushing inland fast and furiously. He stood and said: —

"Flounder, flounder, in the sea,
Quickly, quickly come to me,
For my wife, dame Isabel,
Wishes what I dare not tell."

" Well, what does she wish ? " said the fish.

" Oh dear, she wishes to be king."

" Home with you ; she is king already."

When the man came to the castle he saw that it was now a palace. A herald stood before the door, and a number of soldiers with trumpets.

Inside, everything was of marble and gold. He entered the throne room and there sat his wife upon a throne of gold. She wore a golden crown and held a scepter of pure gold and jewels. ·

The man went up to her and said, " Well, wife, so now you are king ! "

" Yes, now I am king, but I am tired of this already. Go to your fish and tell him that I must be emperor."

" Oh dear ! " said the man, " I cannot do it — I cannot ask him such a thing."

" Now, see here," said the wife ; " I am king ; you are only my husband, so you will go at once ! I will and must be emperor ! "

The fisherman was obliged to go.

When he came to the sea, the water was quite black and thick, and the foam flew and the wind blew. The man was terrified, but he stood and said : —

> "Flounder, flounder, in the sea,
> Quickly, quickly come to me,
> For my wife, dame Isabel,
> Wishes what I dare not tell."

"Well, what is it now ?" said the fish.

"Oh dear, my wife wishes to be emperor."

"Home with you; she is emperor already."

When the man reached home, he found the palace adorned with golden gates. The soldiers were being marshaled before the door. Within, barons and earls and dukes were waiting about like servants.

His wife was sitting on a throne made of one entire piece of gold. She wore a golden crown set with diamonds and rubies. In one hand she held the scepter and in the other the globe.

"Well, wife, so now you are emperor."

"Yes; now I am emperor."

"Well, wife, there is nothing left to be, now you are emperor."

"What are you talking about, husband?" said she. "I am emperor, and next I will be pope. Go and tell the fish so."

"Now, wife," said the man, "how can I ask him such a thing? It is too bad!"

"Rubbish!" said the wife. "Go along and ask him. I am emperor, and you are only my husband, so you must."

He went, feeling much frightened. On the way he shivered and shook, and his knees trembled.

A great wind arose; clouds flew by; the sea rose mountain high; the ships were tossed about; and the sky was dark and red, as in a great tempest. The fisherman stood trembling as he said : —

> " Flounder, flounder, in the sea,
> Quickly, quickly come to me,
> For my wife, dame Isabel,
> Wishes what I dare not tell."

" Well, what now ? " said the fish.

" Oh dear! she wishes to be pope."

" Home with you! She is pope already."

When he reached home, he found himself before a great church, with palaces all round. He had to make his way through a crowd of people.

When he got inside, he found the place lighted up with thousands and thousands of lights. His wife was clothed in a golden garment and sat upon a very high throne. On both sides of her stood two rows of lights of all sizes, and all the emperors and kings were kneeling before her and kissing her foot.

" Well, wife, so you are pope."

" Yes, now I am pope."

" Well, now, wife, what is there left to be,

now you are pope? You can be nothing more."

"We shall see about that," said the wife.

That night the new pope slept little. She tossed and turned from side to side, thinking all the while what she could be next. Nothing occurred to her.

When she saw the red dawn she went to the window to see the sun rise. As it came up, she said, "Ah, I have it! What if I should make the sun and moon to rise! Husband, go to your fish and tell him I want power over the sun and moon."

"Oh, — wife, what did you say?"

"Husband," said she, "if I cannot make the sun and moon rise when I want them, I shall never have another quiet hour. Go to the fish and tell him so."

"O wife," said the man, and fell on his knees to her, "the fish can really not do that for you. I grant he could make you emperor and pope. Be contented with that, I beg of you."

But she became wild with impatience, and screamed out, "I can wait no longer. Go at once!"

Off he went as well as he could for fright. A dreadful storm arose, so that he could hardly keep his feet. Houses and trees were blown down; mountains trembled; and rocks fell into the sea.

He cried out, without being able to hear his own words : —

> "Flounder, flounder, in the sea,
> Quickly, quickly come to me,
> For my wife, dame Isabel,
> Wishes what I dare not tell."

"Well, what now?" asked the flounder.

"Oh dear! She wishes to order about the sun and moon."

"Home with you!" said the flounder. "You will find her in the old hovel."

And there they live to this very day.

— GRIMM.

DISCONTENT

trig   pas'sion   tire'some

Down in a field, one day in June,
    The flowers all bloomed together,
Save one, who tried to hide herself,
    And drooped that pleasant weather.

A robin, who had flown too high,
    And felt a little lazy,
Was resting near a buttercup
    Who wished she were a daisy.

For daisies grow so trig and tall!
    She always had a passion
For wearing frills around her neck,
    In just the daisies' fashion.

And buttercups must always be
  The same old tiresome color;
While daisies dress in gold and white,
  Although their gold is duller.

" Dear Robin," said the sad young flower,
  " Perhaps you'd not mind trying
To find a nice white frill for me,
  Some day when you are flying ? "

" You silly thing ! " the robin said,
  " I think you must be crazy :
I'd rather be my honest self,
  Than any made-up daisy.

" You're nicer in your own bright gown,
  The little children love you ;
Be the best buttercup you can,
  And think no flower above you.

" Though swallows leave me out of sight,
  We'd better keep our places ;
Perhaps the world would all go wrong
  With one too many daisies.

"Look bravely up into the sky,
  And be content with knowing
That God wished for a buttercup
  Just here, where you are growing."

—SARAH ORNE JEWETT.

THE THREE WISHES

dis ap peared'	pro long'	per ceived'
per plexed'	ne'ces sa ry	in'stant ly
qual'i ty	thor'ough ly	prom'ised

There was once a man, not very rich, who
had a pretty woman for his wife. One winter's evening, as he sat by the fire, they
talked of the happiness of their neighbors,
who were richer than they.

Said the wife, " If it were in my power to
have what I wish, I should be happier than
all of them."

"So should I, too," said the husband; " I
wish we had fairies now, and that one of them
would grant me what I might ask."

At that instant they saw a very beautiful

lady in their room, who said, " I am a fairy;
and I promise to grant you the three first
wishes you shall wish. But, take care;
after having wished for three things, I will

not grant one wish further." The fairy disappeared; and the man and his wife were
much perplexed.

"For my own part," said the wife, " if it is
left to my choice, I know very well what I
shall wish for. I do not wish yet, but I
think nothing is so good as to be handsome,
rich, and to be of good quality."

But the husband answered: "With all these things one might be sick, fretful, and one may die young. It would be much wiser to wish for health, cheerfulness, and a long life."

"But of what use is a long life with poverty?" said the wife. "It would only prolong our misery. In truth, the fairy should have promised us a dozen gifts, for there are at least a dozen things which I want."

"That's true," said the husband; "but let us take time. Let us consider, from this time till morning, the three things which are most necessary for us, and then wish."

"I'll think all night," said the wife; "meanwhile, let us warm ourselves, for it is very cold."

At the same time the wife took the tongs to mend the fire. Seeing there were a great many coals thoroughly lighted, she said, without thinking, "Here's a nice fire; I wish we had a yard of black pudding for our supper. We could dress it easily." She had hardly said these words, when down the chimney came tumbling a yard of black pudding for supper.

" Oh, you silly woman," said her husband. " There's a fine wish indeed ! Now we have only two left; for my part, I am so vexed, that I wish the black pudding fast to the tip of your nose."

The man soon perceived that he was sillier than his wife; for at that second wish up starts the black pudding, and sticks so fast to the tip of his poor wife's nose, there was no means to take it off.

" Wretch that I am ! " cried she. " You are a wicked man for wishing the pudding fast to my nose."

" My dear," answered the husband, " I did not think of it; but what shall we do ? I am about wishing for vast riches, and I will have a golden case made to hide the pudding."

" Not at all," answered the wife, " for I should kill myself, were I to live with this pudding dangling at my nose. We have still a wish to make. Leave it to me, or I shall instantly throw myself out of the window." And with this she ran and opened the window.

Her husband, who loved his wife, called out, " Hold, my dear wife; I give you leave to wish for what you will."

" Well," said the wife, " my wish is, that this pudding may fall off."

At that instant the pudding dropped off.

The wife, who did not want for wit, said to her husband, "The fairy was in the right. Let us wish for nothing, and take things as it shall please God to send them. In the meantime, let us sup upon our pudding, since that is all that remains to us of our three wishes."

The husband wisely thought that his wife was right. They supped merrily, and never gave themselves any further trouble about the things which they had meant to wish for.

— C. PERRAULT.

THE WRECK AND THE LIFEBOAT

pas'sen gers   in creased'   ear'nest ly

The storm had increased in fury until the seventh day, when we lost all hope. The crew were worn out by labor and watching. Several leaks appeared, the waves dashed in, and the ship began to fill with water.

My heart sank as I looked at my wife and our four young sons. We knelt down and prayed earnestly to God. Afterwards we felt comforted.

Above the roar of the waves, I heard a cry of " Land, land ! " At the same moment the ship struck against a rock with such force as to throw every one down.

" Lower the boats ! We are lost ! " shouted the captain.

I hurried on deck only to see the last boat leaving the ship. I called at the top of my voice, but no one heard.

I saw, however, that we had still a chance for our lives. Part of the ship was raised above the breakers, and, in the distance, I could see a line of rocky coast.

"Courage," I said. "If the sea calms to-morrow, we may be able to reach the shore."

The children then ate a good supper and soon fell fast asleep.

In the morning I called the boys and we all met on deck.

"Oh, papa!" cried Jack, "where are the sailors and the other passengers?"

"My children," said I, "our friends have left us, but God will help us. Let us think what is best to be done."

"Could we not make a raft, papa?" said Ernest.

"That would be a good plan," I replied, "if we had anything to make it with."

"We might swim to the shore," said Fritz, the eldest; "the sea is quite calm."

"That is all very well for you, who can swim," said Ernest. "But we can't."

"Well," said I, "suppose we look through the ship to see what we can find."

Away we all went in different directions. Jack took his way toward the captain's cabin. The moment he opened the door two large dogs jumped out. How glad they were to be free! They bounded so with delight that they knocked little Jack head over heels.

But Jack was on his feet again in an instant. He seized one of the dogs by the ears, jumped on his back, and rode up to me. How I laughed at the sight!

We gathered in the cabin to tell what we had found. Fritz had found two guns, some shot, powder, and bullets. Ernest showed a cap full of nails, an ax, a saw, and a hammer. Little Franz, the youngest, carried a box of sharp fishing hooks.

"You have all done well," said I; "but I am afraid Jack's dogs will eat more than any of us. Besides, they will be of little use."

"Oh, papa," cried Jack, "they will help us to hunt."

"That is, in case we ever get ashore. But how can that be done?"

"Could we not sail in tubs?" said Jack. "I have often sailed in a tub on the pond at home."

"A good thought!" cried I. "Let us see if we can find any tubs."

We soon found four large iron-bound casks. These I sawed through the middle, making two tubs out of each cask. These I set in a row near the edge of the water.

Next we got a long, slender plank and set the tubs upon it. The ends of the plank were bent so as to make a keel. I nailed two other planks to the tubs on each side, bringing the ends together to form bow and stern.

We pushed our little craft into the water, but she leaned too far to one side. We threw in some heavy things and the boat righted itself.

The boys were eager to start at once, but I forbade them. It was too late in the day to make the attempt. So, for one night more, we slept in our hammocks on the wreck.

—JOHANN DAVID WYSS.

THE CARPENTER

meas'ured car'pen ter per'fect ly joints

I thought I could saw, and I thought I could
  plane,
And I thought I was clever with nails,
And I mended a chair (though it's broken
  again),
And I once made a couple of bails.

But directly the car-
  penter came to
  our house
To put up some
  shelves in the
  hall,
And I sat by his
  side just as still
  as a mouse,
I knew I knew nothing at all.

He measured each part with the greatest of
  care,
(A foot rule's a thing I don't use),

He labored to make the joints perfectly square,
And he always bored holes for the screws.

Now it's all very well to go hammering round,
And to look on a tool chest as fun;
But in future my carpenter work shall be
    sound,
And done once for all, if it's done.

—E. Lucas.

GOING ASHORE

| fla min'goes | mas'tiffs | pen'guins | tack'le |
| can'vas | Franz | Fritz | cou'ple |

Next morning we all rose early.

"Let the poor animals we leave behind be well fed," said I. "Put plenty of food near them also. In a few days we may be able to return for them. Then gather all the stores you can think of."

The boys joyfully obeyed. From what they brought, I chose canvas to make a tent, a chest of carpenter's tools, fishing rod and tackle, an iron pot, and cases of meat jelly and biscuit.

189

With a prayer to God we now took our places, each in one of the tubs. Just then we heard the cocks crow.

"Why should not the fowls go with us?"

I cried. "If we fail to find food for them, they can at least be food for us."

Ten hens and a couple of cocks were placed in one of the tubs. The ducks, geese, and pigeons were set at liberty. The ducks and geese took to the water, while the pigeons flew swiftly toward the shore.

Now we moved slowly from the wreck. My wife sat in the front. Next her was Franz, a pretty boy nearly eight years old. Next came Fritz, a handsome, manly lad of fifteen. The two center tubs held our cargo. Then came Jack, and next him Ernest, the second son. I guided the raft from the stern, while the elder boys rowed.

We had left behind two large mastiffs, Turk and Juno. They would have been too heavy for our frail raft. But when they saw us leaving, they sprang into the sea and followed.

Many casks and boxes floated on the water near us. Fritz and I secured a couple of hogsheads. "Perhaps they may contain food," said I. "Everything is of value just now."

The nearer we came to the shore, the more barren it looked. But after a time green trees were seen.

"See those palm trees, papa," cried Fritz. "I am certain they are palms."

"If they are only cocoa palms," sighed Ernest, "how happy we all should be to drink the delicious milk!"

Our geese and ducks were swimming toward an opening in the rocks. Here a stream flowed into the sea. We followed and found ourselves in a small bay.

As soon as our boat touched the shore, every one sprang out but little Franz. He was lifted out by his mother.

The dogs received us with loud barks of delight. The geese and ducks cackled loudly, while the cries of the flamingoes and penguins added to the uproar.

We first knelt to thank God for our escape. Then we went in search of a good tenting ground. We found a pleasant spot and at once pitched the tent.

When this had been done, the boys ran to collect moss and grass to spread in the tent for our beds. Meanwhile I built a fireplace with large, flat stones from the stream.

Dry twigs and seaweed were soon blazing on the hearth. My wife, with the help of little Franz, prepared supper.

After a good meal we were all ready for rest. We closed our tent door, and slept sweetly on rude beds of grass and moss.

COCOANUTS, SUGAR CANES, AND MONKEYS

ex pe di'tion	wea'pon	jab'ber ing
pe cul'iar	de scend'ed	need'less ly

After our first breakfast on shore, it was decided that Fritz and I should start on an exploring expedition.

We armed ourselves with guns, a pair of pistols, and a small hatchet. We took biscuits, part of the lobster, and a flask of water and started off, followed by our trusty dog Turk.

We turned our steps toward the seashore, which we soon reached. Then we pushed on until we came to a pleasant grove. Here we halted to rest, sitting under a large tree.

Fritz thought he saw a monkey among the branches. He started up and went to the other side of the tree to look. In doing so he stumbled over something round, which he picked up and brought to me.

"Is this a peculiar sort of bird's nest?" he asked.

"No," laughed I. "It is a cocoanut."

We split open the nut, but the kernel was dry and uneatable.

"I always thought," cried Fritz, "that a cocoanut was full of sweet liquid like milk."

"So it is," I replied, "when young and fresh. As it ripens, however, the milk thickens, and in course of time hardens into a kernel. When the nut falls on favorable soil, the germ within the kernel swells until it bursts through the shell. Then it takes root and begins to grow."

"I do not understand," said Fritz, "how the little plant gets through this thick shell."

"Trust Nature," I answered. "Look here. Do you see these three round holes near the stalk? It is through them that the plantlet gets out."

Our way now led through a thicket so densely overgrown with creeping plants that we were forced to use our hatchet to open a path.

Presently we descended a hill. At a little distance was a clump of palm trees. To reach them we had to pass through a dense thicket of weeds, where I feared at every step that we might tread on a snake.

I sent Turk in advance. Then I cut one of the reeds, thinking it would be a useful weapon against a snake. I had carried it but a little way, when I noticed a thick juice coming from one end. I tasted it, and found it sweet and pleasant. I knew then that I was standing amongst sugar canes.

"Fritz must make the same discovery," thought I. So I said aloud, "Fritz, cut yourself a cane, for we may meet a snake."

He did so, and as he walked he beat the canes with it right and left. Presently it split, and he found his hand covered with juice.

He carefully touched the cane with the tip of his tongue. Finding the juice sweet, he tasted it again.

"Oh, father, sugar canes! sugar canes!" he cried. "We must take a lot home with us."

He cut a dozen of the largest and tucked them under his arm. We then pushed through the canebrake and reached the clump of palms.

Immediately a troop of monkeys sprang

up, jabbering at us and grinding their teeth. Before we could see them clearly, they had darted to the very top of the cocoanut trees. Fritz was so provoked that he raised his gun and would have shot one of the poor beasts.

"Stay!" cried I. "Never take the life of any animal needlessly. A live monkey up in that tree is of more use than a dozen dead ones at our feet. See!"

I had gathered a handful of small stones, which I now threw up at the monkeys. The stones did not go near them, but the little creatures became very angry. They seized all the cocoanuts within their reach and sent a perfect hail of them down upon us.

Fritz laughed with delight as he picked up some of the finest of the nuts. We drank the milk by drawing it through the holes which we had pierced in the shell. Afterwards we split the nuts open with the hatchet and ate the cream which lined the shells. —JOHANN DAVID WYSS.

THE CAPTAIN'S DAUGHTER

shat'tered   rat'tling   stag'gered
an'chored   break'ers   shud'dered

We were crowded in the cabin,
  Not a soul would dare to sleep, —
It was midnight on the waters,
  And a storm was on the deep.

'Tis a fearful thing in winter,
  To be shattered by the blast,
And to hear the rattling trumpet
  Thunder, "Cut away the mast!"

So we shuddered there in silence, —
  For the stoutest held his breath,
While the hungry sea was roaring,
  And the breakers talked with Death.

As thus we sat in darkness,
  Each one busy with his prayers,
"We are lost!" the captain shouted,
  As he staggered down the stairs.

But his little daughter whispered,
  As she took his icy hand,
"Isn't God upon the ocean,
  Just the same as on the land?"

Then we kissed the little maiden,
  And we spoke in better cheer,
And we anchored safe in harbor
  When the morn was shining clear.
          — JAMES T. FIELDS.

ARTHUR AND THE SWORD

tour'ney	en chant'er	ad vised'	Ec'tor
U'ther	arch bish'op	Can'ter bur y	to'ken

Fourteen hundred years ago there were sad times in England. The King, Uther Pendragon, was dead. His little son, who should have been king in his stead, had disappeared.

No one knew where the prince was. Some believed that the secret was known to Merlin, the old enchanter. But when the boldest asked him, he shook his white head and answered never a word.

In those days there were very few laws. The rich lords fought each other; they were cruel to the poor. Every year the rich grew more savage and the poor more wretched.

Now the head of the church was the Archbishop of Canterbury. He was a good man, and full of pity for both rich and poor.

"England needs a king," he said to Merlin. "Can you not help to find one for her?"

"Call all the nobles to St. Paul's on Christmas Day," advised Merlin. "There shall they learn who shall be king."

So the nobles of England rode to London and heard mass in the great church on Christmas Day. As they left the church, they saw a strange sight.

In the churchyard stood a huge stone, crossed by a bar of steel. In the steel was held by the sharp point a wonderful shining sword. About the sword were gold letters. The knights drew near and read: "Whoso pulleth out this sword shall be king of England."

They looked at one another in awe for a moment. Then they each attempted to draw the sword. Strong men tugged and pulled, but to no purpose. Not a noble could draw the sword.

The archbishop was content, for he knew that no knight there could rule himself. So, of course, he could not rule England.

"The king is not here," said the archbishop, "but in good time God will make him known. Meanwhile, let us set a guard of ten knights about the stone." And it was done.

On New Year's Day there was to be a tourney. Among those who came to London was a brave knight, Sir Ector. With him were his son, Sir Kay, and Kay's foster brother, Arthur.

As they rode, Kay suddenly found that he had forgotten his sword.

"Arthur," he said, "I pray you to ride back for my sword."

Arthur hastened home, but the house was locked. Every one had gone to the tourney.

"Shall Kay lack a sword to-day?" cried Arthur. "Never! I will take the one from St. Paul's Churchyard first."

The stone was unguarded, for the ten knights were on their way to the tourney with all the rest of the world.

The lightest touch drew the sword from its place. It was Arthur's!

He never stopped to read the gold writing, but hastened to give the sword to Kay.

Sir Kay knew the sword at once. He rode to Sir Ector and showed him the wonderful token. "Father, now am I king of England."

But Sir Ector doubted. He led both the young men to the church and, before the high altar, he questioned Kay. "My brother Arthur gave me the sword," admitted the young knight.

"I will show you where I found it," said Arthur. He led them to the rock and placed the point of the sword as before. Instantly it was held as by grips of steel. Neither Sir

Ector nor Sir Kay could take again the sword.

"Now, Arthur," said Sir Ector.

At the lad's touch, the sword came forth as lightly as a feather.

Sir Ector and Sir Kay fell upon their knees.

"Why do you kneel to me, father?" cried Arthur. "I like it not."

"I kneel to my king and England's," said Sir Ector. "You are not my son, although I have loved you as a son.

"Years ago Merlin brought you to me, a little, helpless babe. Now I know you for the son of Uther Pendragon."

The nobles and the people were gathered

together. When it was seen that Arthur
alone could move the sword, the people cried:
"Long live King Arthur! He and he only
shall be our king!"

Then Arthur was made a knight. Then
the archbishop set the crown upon his bright
hair, and there he promised to be a true king
and to deal wisely and justly all his days.
And this great pledge he faithfully kept.

ARTHUR AND THE SWORD EXCALIBUR

Ex cal′i bur van′ished con di′tion Pel′li nore
scab′bard   com′bat   vic′tor   daz′zling

King Arthur did not hold himself above
the combat. He loved to cross swords on a
fair field with any good knight. Usually the
king was the victor, but at rare times he met
his match.

Once was when he faced Sir Pellinore.
There was a long, fierce fight between them,
until Pellinore smote Arthur's sword in two
pieces.

"Yield thee!" cried the knight. "Yield, or I will slay thee."

"Death is welcome," said Arthur. "I would die rather than yield." With these words he rushed on the knight, seized him about the waist, and threw him down.

But Pellinore arose again and would have slain Arthur, had not Merlin appeared.

"Stay!" cried Merlin. "This knight is one greater than thou thinkest."

"Why, who is he?" asked Sir Pellinore.

"Thy king!"

Then Sir Pellinore, afraid because of what he had done, tried yet harder to slay Arthur. Merlin, however, cast a spell upon him so that he fell to the earth in a great sleep.

Arthur thought him dead. "Merlin, why hast thou destroyed this good knight?" he cried. "He was mine own fair foe."

"Fear not, Arthur," answered the sage. "He shall rise up again in three hours."

Then Merlin guided Arthur to the home of

a hermit. This hermit tended his wounds, and in three days he was healed.

Then said the king to Merlin, "I have no sword."

"Thou shalt have one in due season."

So they rode for hours until they reached the shores of a wonderful lake In the midst of the lake the king saw an arm rising above the water and holding aloft a sword.

"Behold the sword," said Merlin.

Arthur looked again and saw a maiden in white coming toward him.

"This is the Lady of the Lake," said Merlin. "The sword is hers. Speak fairly to her, and she may give it to you."

"Maiden," said Arthur, "whose sword is this I see? I would it were mine, for I have lost my sword."

"Thou shalt have the sword, King Arthur, on one condition. It is that you will give me a gift when I ask it."

"By my word," said Arthur. "Thou shalt have whatever gift thou shalt ask."

"Close at hand is a barge," said the Lady of the Lake. "Row out and take Excalibur, but forget not the scabbard also."

King Arthur and Merlin tied their horses safely and paddled out to the center of the lake. When Arthur took the sword by the hilt, the arm vanished.

As they rode on their way, Arthur often looked with joy at his new sword. Excalibur was indeed beautiful. The hilt was rich with dazzling jewels, and the blade was so bright that its light blinded the eyes of men.

"Which dost thou like the better?" asked Merlin, "the sword or the scabbard?"

" The sword," replied Arthur.

" You are not wise. The scabbard is worth ten such swords. Keep it by you always. For as long as it is buckled on you, you will lose no blood, however sorely you are wounded."

Thus came King Arthur by his famous sword Excalibur.

THE SETTING UP OF THE ROUND TABLE

Cam'e lot	hom'age
Guin'e vere	Le'o de grance

King Arthur came to Merlin one day and said, " My barons bid me take a wife. What is thy advice ? "

" The thought is a good one," said Merlin. " Is there any woman whom you love ? "

" Yes," said Arthur, " I love Guinevere, the daughter of King Leodegrance. To him my father gave a Round Table. Guinevere is the fairest maiden that I have ever seen."

" She is beautiful, indeed," said Merlin.

" But I can find you a maiden as fair, and one of greater goodness. But I see your heart is set."

So Merlin, with a fair company of knights, rode to ask King Leodegrance for the hand of his daughter.

"This is good news," said the king. "Little did I think that the great King Arthur would wish to marry my child. As a wedding gift I shall send him what he will value more than lands or treasure. I shall send him the Round Table that Uther Pendragon gave me. There are places at the table for one hundred and fifty knights. Once I had that goodly number, but the wars have slain fifty. However, the hundred shall go with Guinevere."

When Arthur heard the king's answer, he said, " This is good news indeed. I have long loved Guinevere, and I value the Round Table more than great riches."

Then Merlin sought fifty brave and famous knights through the length and breadth of

Sir Galahad.

England. But he only found eight and twenty.

The Round Table was set up at Camelot. The Archbishop of Canterbury came to bless the seats that were placed around the table.

After the blessing, Arthur entered.

"Rise, fair Sirs," said Merlin, "and pay your homage to the king."

Afterwards it was seen that the name of every knight was written in his seat in letters of gold. But two of the seats bore no names.

"Why are these places empty?" asked the king of Merlin.

"No man save the worthiest may sit in these seats. One is the Seat Perilous. There only one man in the whole earth shall be found worthy to sit."

Then Merlin took Sir Pellinore by the hand and placed him next the Perilous Seat. "This is your place," he said; "for of all here you are the most worthy." This was the same Sir Pellinore who had well-nigh slain the king.

Next day King Arthur wedded Guinevere.

The knights of the Round Table were there, rejoicing in their vows to the king. They had laid aside their armor and were robed in white. It was a day of holy joy to all. Thus was set up the Table Round in Camelot.

SEVEN TIMES ONE ARE SEVEN

col'um bine   cuck'oo pint   marsh'ma ry

There's no dew left on the daisies and clover,
   There's no rain left in heaven;
I've said my " seven times " over and over,
   Seven times one are seven.

I am old, so old I can write a letter;
   My birthday lessons are done;
The lambs play always, they know no better;
   They are only one times one.

O moon! in the night I have seen you sailing
   And shining so round and low;
You were bright! ah, bright! but your light
   is failing, —
   You are nothing now but a bow.

You moon, have you done something wrong
    in heaven
  That God has hidden your face?
I hope if you have you will soon be forgiven
  And shine again in your place.

O velvet bee, you're a dusty fellow;
  You've powdered your legs with gold!
O brave marshmary buds, rich and yellow,
  Give me your money to hold!

O columbine, open your folded wrapper,
  Where two twin turtledoves dwell!
O cuckoopint, toll me the purple clapper
  That hangs in your clear green bell!

And show me your nest, with the young ones
    in it, —
  I will not steal it away;
I am old! you may trust me, linnet, linnet, —
  I am seven times one to-day.

                — JEAN INGELOW.

THE NECKLACE OF TRUTH

| ad mi ra'tion | am'e thyst |
| Cor'a lie | mag nif'i cent |

Once there was a little girl named Coralie. She had but one fault. She told falsehoods.

Her parents tried to cure her in many ways, but in vain. Finally they decided to take her to the enchanter Merlin.

The enchanter Merlin lived in a glass palace. He loved truth. He knew liars by their odor a league off. When Coralie came toward the castle, Merlin was forced to burn vinegar to keep himself from being ill.

Coralie's mother began to explain the reason for their coming. But Merlin stopped her.

"I know all about your daughter, my good lady," he said. "She is one of the greatest liars in the world. She often makes me ill."

Merlin's face looked so stern that Coralie hid her face under her mother's cloak. Her father stood before her to keep her from harm.

"Do not fear," said Merlin. "I am not going to hurt your little girl. I only wish to make her a present."

He opened a drawer and took from it a magnificent amethyst necklace. It was fastened with a shining clasp of diamonds.

Merlin put the necklace on Coralie's neck and said, "Go in peace, my friends. Your little daughter carries with her a sure guardian of the truth."

Then he looked sternly at Coralie and said,

"In a year I shall come for my necklace. Do not dare to take it off for a single moment. If you do, harm will come to you!"

"Oh, I shall always love to wear it! It is so beautiful!" cried Coralie.

This is the way she came by the wonderful Necklace of Truth.

The day after Coralie returned home she was sent to school. As she had long been absent, the little girls crowded round her. There was a cry of admiration at sight of the necklace.

"Where did it come from? Where did you get it?" they asked.

"I was sick for a long time," replied Coralie. "When I got well, Mamma and Papa gave me the necklace."

A loud cry rose from all at once. The diamonds of the clasp had grown dim. They now looked like coarse glass.

"Yes, indeed, I have been sick! What are you making such a fuss about?"

At this second falsehood the amethysts, in

turn, changed to ugly yellow stones. A new cry arose. Coralie was frightened at the strange behavior of her necklace.

"I have been to the enchanter Merlin," she said very humbly.

Immediately the necklace looked as beautiful as ever. But the children teased her.

"You need not laugh," said Coralie, "for Merlin was very glad to see us. He sent his carriage to the next town to meet us. Such a splendid carriage, with six white horses, pink satin cushions, and a negro coachman with powdered hair. Merlin's palace is all of jasper and gold. He met us at the door and led us to the dining room. There stood a long table covered with delicious things to eat. First of all we ate — "

Coralie stopped, for the children were laughing till the tears rolled down their cheeks. She glanced at her necklace and shuddered. With each new falsehood, the necklace had become longer and longer, till it already dragged on the ground.

"Coralie, you are stretching the truth," cried the girls.

"Well, I confess it. We walked, and we stayed there only five minutes."

The necklace shrunk at once to its proper size.

"The necklace — the necklace — where did it come from?"

"He gave it to me without saying a word. I think —"

She had not time to finish. The fatal necklace grew shorter and shorter till it choked her. She gasped for breath.

"You are keeping back part of the truth," cried her schoolmates.

"He said — that I was — one of the greatest — liars in the world."

The necklace loosened about her neck, but Coralie still cried with pain.

"That was why Merlin gave me the necklace. He said that it would make me truthful. What a fool I have been to be proud of it!"

Her playmates were sorry for her. "If I were in your place," said one of them, "I should send back the necklace. Why do you not take it off?"

Poor Coralie did not wish to speak. The stones, however, began to dance up and down and to make a terrible clatter.

"There is something that you have not told us," laughed the little girls.

"I like to wear it."

Oh, how the diamonds and amethysts danced! It was worse than ever.

"Tell us the reason you are hiding."

"Well, I see I can hide nothing. Merlin forbade me to take it off. He said great harm would come if I disobeyed."

Thanks to the enchanted necklace, Coralie became a truthful child. Long before the year had passed, Merlin came for his necklace. He needed it for another child who told falsehoods.

No one can tell to-day what has become of the wonderful Necklace of Truth. But if I

were a little child in the habit of telling falsehoods, I should not feel quite sure that it
might not be found again some fine day.

— Adapted from MACÉ'S FAIRY BOOK.

DAVID AND GOLIATH

as sayed'	eph'ah	pre vail'
Beth'le hem	Go li'ath	shek'els
cham'pi on	dis dained'	Phi lis'tines
coun'te nance	Ek'ron	cu'bits

Now the Philistines gathered together
their armies to battle.

And the Philistines stood on a mountain
on the one side, and Israel stood on a mountain on the other side: and there was a valley
between them.

And there went out a champion out of the
camp of the Philistines, named Goliath of
Gath, whose height was six cubits and a span.

And he had a helmet of brass upon his
head, and he was armed with a coat of mail;
and the weight of the coat was five thousand
shekels of brass.

And his spear's head weighed six hundred shekels of iron: and one bearing a shield went before him.

And he stood and cried unto the armies of Israel, and said unto them, Why are you come out to set your battle in array? Am not I a Philistine, and ye servants to Saul? Choose you a man for you, and let him come down to me.

If he be able to fight with me, and to kill me, then will we be your servants: but if I prevail against him and kill him, then shall ye be our servants and serve us.

When Saul and all Israel heard these words of the Philistines, they were dismayed and greatly afraid.

Now David was the son of Jesse; and Jesse had eight sons:

And the three eldest sons of Jesse went and followed Saul to the battle;

And David was the youngest: he fed his father's sheep at Bethlehem.

And Jesse said unto David his son, Take

now for thy brethren an ephah of this parched corn, and these ten loaves, and run to the camp to thy brethren;

And carry these ten cheeses unto the captain of their thousand, and look how thy brethren fare, and take their pledge.

And David rose up early in the morning, and left the sheep with a keeper, and took, and went, as Jesse had commanded him; and he came to the trench, as the host was going forth to the fight, and shouted for the battle.

And David left his carriage in the hand of the keeper of the carriage, and ran into the army, and came and saluted his brethren.

And as he talked with them, behold, there came up the champion (the Philistine of Gath, Goliath by name) out of the armies of the Philistines, and spake according to the same words: and David heard them.

And all the men of Israel, when they saw the man, fled from him, and were sore afraid.

And David said to Saul, Let no man's

"There came a lion . . . and took a lamb out of the flock."

heart fail because of him; thy servant will go and fight with this Philistine.

And Saul said to David, Thou art not able to go against this Philistine to fight with him: for thou art but a youth, and he a man of war from his youth.

And David said unto Saul, Thy servant kept his father's sheep, and there came a lion and a bear, and took a lamb out of the flock;

And I went out after him, and smote him, and delivered it out of his mouth: and when he arose against me, I caught him by his beard, and smote him, and slew him.

David said moreover, The Lord that delivered me out of the paw of the lion, and out of the paw of the bear, he will deliver me out of the hand of this Philistine. And Saul said unto David, Go, and the Lord be with thee.

And Saul armed David with his armor, and he put a helmet of brass upon his head; also he armed him with a coat of mail.

And David girded his sword upon his armor, and he assayed to go ; for he had not proved it. And David said unto Saul, I cannot go with these; for I have not proved them. And David put them off him.

And he took his staff in his hand, and chose him five smooth stones out of the brook, and put them in a shepherd's bag which he had, even in a scrip; and his sling was in his hand: and he drew near the Philistine.

And the Philistine came on and drew near unto David; and the man that bear the shield went before him.

And when the Philistine looked about and saw David, he disdained him ; for he was but a youth and ruddy and of fair countenance.

And the Philistine said unto David, Am I a dog that thou comest to me with stones? And the Philistine cursed David by his gods.

And the Philistine said to David, Come to me and I will give thy flesh to the fowls of the air and to the beasts of the fields.

Then said David to the Philistine, Thou comest to me with a sword and with a spear and with a shield; but I come to thee in the name of the Lord of hosts, the God of the armies of Israel, whom thou hast defied.

This day will the Lord deliver thee into mine hand; and I will smite thee, and take thine head from thee; and I will give the carcases of the host of the Philistines this day unto the fowls of the air, and to the wild beasts of the earth; that all the earth may know that there is a God in Israel.

And all the assembly shall know that the Lord saveth not with sword and spear: for the battle is the Lord's and he will give you into our hands.

And it came to pass, when the Philistine arose, and came and drew nigh to meet David, that David hasted, and ran toward the army to meet the Philistine.

And David put his hand in his bag, and took thence a stone, and slang it, and smote the Philistine in his forehead, that the stone

David.

sunk into his forehead; and he fell upon his face to the earth.

So David prevailed over the Philistine with

a sling and with a stone, and smote the Philistine, and slew him; but there was no sword in the hand of David.

Therefore David ran and stood upon the Philistine, and took his sword, and drew it out of the sheath thereof, and slew him, and cut off his head therewith. And when the Philistines saw their champion was dead, they fled.

And the men of Israel and of Judah arose and shouted and pursued the Philistines, until thou come to the valley, and to the gates of Ekron: and the wounded of the Philistines fell down by the way.

And David took the head of the Philistine, and brought it to Jerusalem.   — THE BIBLE.

A PSALM OF DAVID

a noint′est   psalm   right′eous ness

The Lord is my shepherd, I shall not want.

He maketh me to lie down in green pastures : he leadeth me beside the still waters.

(228)   The Good Shepherd.

He restoreth my soul: he leadeth me in the paths of righteousness for his name's sake.

Yea, though I walk through the valley of the shadow of death, I will fear no evil: for thou art with me; thy rod and thy staff they comfort me.

Thou preparest a table before me in the presence of mine enemies; thou anointest my head with oil; my cup runneth over.

Surely goodness and mercy shall follow me all the days of my life; and I will dwell in the house of the Lord for ever. —THE BIBLE.

THE GAME OF HY SPY

Aa'ron	dis sat'is fied	mar'tyrs
ben'e fit	ex pe'ri ence	re leased'
çau'tious ly	in cau'tious	rec on noi'ter ing
in fe'ri or	re solved'	so lem'ni ty
dis cov'er y	ven'tured	sat'is fied
a gree'a bly	ex act'ness	com'ic al

The children went out on the barn floor and stood in a semicircle, while Ralph re-

peated with much solemnity and exact-
ness,—

> "Eggs, cheese, butter, bread,
> Stick, stock, stone dead."

to see who would be " it."

Ralph said this over and over, till every one
was out but Teddy.

"There," said Ralph, "Teddy is *it*. Now,
Teddy, don't you count too fast. Count out
loud, so we can hear you."

Teddy hid his face on the post by the horse
manger, and began counting very loud and

fast, so that it sounded almost like one word. There was a great deal of tittering and scampering about.

"Ninety-eight — ninety-nine — one-hundred!" shouted Teddy, whirling round.

The barn was still as night. Old Kate blinked over the manger at him in a wise way, as much as to say, "I know, but I shan't tell."

Teddy looked sharply all around, keeping hold of the post with one hand. What was that bit of red, down by the east haymow? He went a little nearer.

"Touch the goal for Lois and Millie!" shouted Teddy, rushing back.

"Touch the goal for my own self!" cried Roy, hopping out of the horse manger and clasping the post before Teddy could reach it.

Lois and Millie crawled out of a hole in the haymow, with hair full of hayseed and bits of straw.

"How did you know where we were?" asked Lois.

"I saw a piece of Millie's dress, and I knew

of course you two'd be together. But now, where's that long-legged Ralph, I wonder?"

Every one looked wise and important, as if nothing would induce him to tell. Teddy pried about, making longer and longer sallies from his post, trying to have eyes all over his head at once. The girls tittered and looked down the bay towards the cow stable. Teddy ventured a little farther that way, when lo! Ralph swung himself down plump from the scaffolding overhead, and with long strides made the goal before Teddy could by any means get there.

Now it was Millie's turn to be "it." Millie resolved to be very sharp, and not let the boys outwit her. She kept close by the post, reconnoitering the barn in all directions for some signs of the enemy. What was that small bunch projecting from the big beam overhead? Was it a knot, or a swallow's nest, or what was it?

She tiptoed cautiously out for a better view. Ha! it moved, it was the toe of a boot.

Whose boot, was now the question. If she called the wrong name, she would lose all the benefit of the discovery. It must be Ralph or Roy. Teddy couldn't get up there. As she watched, an incautious elbow was also projected. There was no mistaking the patch on that elbow.

"Touch the goal for Roy Whittaker!" shouted Millie.

"It isn't fair. You didn't see me," said Roy, thrusting his head over the beam.

"I did, too. You stuck over so I couldn't help it."

"I kept telling you she'd see us, if you didn't lie stiller," said a smothered voice from the beam.

"Touch the goal for Ralph," cried Millie.

Ralph and Roy climbed down, much dissatisfied with each other. Ralph said Roy wriggled about like an eel, and spoilt all their fun; and Roy said of course such an old spindle-shanks as Ralph could hide behind a half-foot beam easy enough. There might have been a serious quarrel, but just then loud cries were heard from Tom's manger.

"Oh, come here! Come quick!" said the voice in tones of distress.

Lois had hid in Tom's manger, and, being covered with hay, Tom, in taking some hay, had helped himself to a mouthful of Lois's hair. This he was proceeding to munch. The boys went to the rescue. Lois was soon released, half laughing, half frightened.

When Roy began to count, Millie whispered to Lois and Teddy, —

"I've thought of a first-rate place for us three, where Roy won't think of looking, I know. Let's all hide in the grain bin."

The grain bin was only partly filled with oats. By climbing upon the half-bushel measure, then upon a barrel, they reached the top. Then it was easy enough to hop in. Millie dropped the cover carefully down after her as she jumped in, and there the three were as snug as possible.

It was great fun to hear Roy prowling

about outside, wondering where they could be. Meanwhile they were sitting inside on the oats, nudging each other, and holding their mouths to keep from giggling aloud.

By and by Roy thought of the grain bin, and lifted the cover. Three jolly faces, red with laughter, greeted his eyes. He dropped the cover and ran to touch the goal. Loud cries were now heard from the grain bin.

"Roy! Roy! Come and help us! We can't get the cover up."

Roy went back.

"Well, you *are* in a nice fix! I don't see how you'll ever get out of here. I don't believe you ever can."

After teasing them awhile, Roy went to work, with Ralph's help, to get them out. But the slippery oats slid and gave way, and filled their shoes full. The more they struggled to get out, the deeper they sank.

Finally Ralph and Roy went to tell mother. Millie, Lois, and Teddy sat down on the oats, looking rather sober.

"We shouldn't starve to death, if we had to stay here all night," said Teddy, "because we could eat oats like the horses."

They all tried the oats and found them a prickly, tasteless food, decidedly inferior even to plain bread and butter.

"Prisoners feel just as we do now," said Millie. "Let's play we are prisoners."

"Play we're put in here because we're so good, like the martyrs in grandma's book," said Lois.

Millie and Teddy were both agreeably struck with the idea.

"How do folks act when they're so good?" asked Lois. "I don't know how to begin."

"Oh, you must look like this," said Millie, drawing down the corners of her mouth and raising her eyebrows. "Of course we feel dreadful to be treated so, just because we're so good. Now we must all sigh."

They all heaved a loud sigh. Then they burst out laughing, for their faces were so comical with this new expression.

"I suppose they'll come and take us out, to saw us in two, to-morrow," observed Teddy.

"Oh Teddy, don't talk so! You make me scrooge all over," said Lois.

"Oh, you needn't be afraid. I shall fight them all, and take you and Millie right on my horse, and ride right away with you through the middle of them."

Here footsteps were heard, and soon Aaron, the hired man, looked over into the bin.

"Hello!" said Aaron; "there are the biggest rats I ever caught in my grain bin."

Aaron put the half-bushel measure in for them to stand on. Then he took them, one by one, in his strong hands, and swung them out upon the floor.

The young martyrs scampered off for the house, quite satisfied with even this short experience of prison life.

— MARY PRUDENCE WELLS SMITH.

APOLLO AND HYACINTHUS

A pol'lo   hy'a cinth   op por tu'ni ty .
dis'cus   Hy a cinth'us   quoits
es pe'cial   mar'vel ous   stanch
jeal'ous   mel'o dy   Zeph'y rus

Apollo was one of the most beautiful of the
Greek gods. He had fair curling hair and

Apollo.

large blue eyes.
He was also very
strong. He was
a famous hunter,
for no one could
shoot arrows
so far and so
straight.

Apollo was
also a wonderful
musician. He
played on a lyre,
which is a kind

of harp. Even the gods themselves would
stop work or play to listen to Apollo's music.

Apollo had one dear friend named Hyacinthus. Hyacinthus was a youth who loved all manly sports. Apollo spent most of his days with his friend.

When Hyacinthus hunted on the mountains, Apollo led the dogs to the chase. When Hyacinthus fished in the deep lake, Apollo tended the lines and hauled the nets. Always, the sport was good when Apollo was with Hyacinthus.

In the cool of evening, after the day of toil, Apollo would take his lyre and play to his friend.

Hyacinthus loved all Apollo's music, but one melody he loved especially. It was a song that was sad but very sweet. It had no words.

" Why has that song no words, Apollo ? " asked Hyacinthus.

" I cannot tell. Words fail me when I try to fit them to this song, Hyacinthus," Apollo answered.

" Some day you will find words ? "

And Apollo answered, " Some day."

These two friends had one enemy and they knew it not. This was Zephyrus, the west wind. He had loved Hyacinthus and had longed to be his dearest friend. But Hyacinthus loved Apollo best.

Zephyrus became very jealous. He resolved to put an end to this friendship which angered him so greatly. And one day his opportunity came.

It was late in the afternoon. Apollo and Hyacinthus were resting after a ramble in the hills. Suddenly Apollo sprang to his feet. " I am for quoits," he cried ; and seizing the discus he threw it high and far.

Hyacinthus ran to seize it, eager to show his strength and skill.

This was the chance that the evil Zephyrus had sought. He breathed upon the falling quoit, and the huge stone bounded aside and struck Hyacinthus a blow on the temple.

The poor youth fell to the ground.

Apollo, pale as Hyacinthus himself, hastened to the side of his friend. He raised

241

him in his arms, he tried to stanch the wound, but all was in vain. The head of the beautiful lad fell weakly over on the shoulder of the god.

"Hyacinthus," cried Apollo, "thou art dying, and I am the cause. Would that I could die for thee!"

"Hyacinthus," cried Apollo again, "thou shalt not die in memory, for I have now the words of thy favorite song. Grief has taught them to me."

And Hyacinthus smiled as he died.

As Apollo gazed at his friend, he said, "Thou shalt become a flower!" And lo! the blood of Hyacinthus was changed to a tall and lily-like flower of deepest crimson.

On its petals Apollo wrote, so that all might read, "Ah! ah!" And these words of mourning we read on the hyacinth to this day.

But the wonderful melody with the still more marvelous words is sung no more on the earth. Mortals hear that now in their hearts only as grief draws near. — Fanny E. Coe.

COE'S THIRD R. — 16

THE WONDERFUL RIDE OF PHAETON

char'i ot   dis as'ter   per sist'ed   Ju'pi ter
Nep'tune   Pha'e ton   dif'fi cult   pal'ace

Apollo was not only god of music and of the chase; he was also god of the sun. Every day, he rode through the sky in his golden chariot drawn by fiery horses. On his head was a crown from which shot dazzling rays of light.

Each morning, Apollo left the great sun palace in India to set out on his daily journey. Each evening he watered his weary steeds in the western ocean.

Apollo had a son named Phaeton. One day Phaeton had pleased his father by a bold deed. Apollo said, "My son, I am pleased with you. Ask anything, and I will grant it."

"Let me drive your chariot for one day, my father," cried Phaeton.

"My son, I dare not grant your request. It would be too dangerous. The road is steep and difficult; the horses are quite untamed;

even I, at times, grow fearful. What would become of you, a mortal? You would grow dizzy and fall."

But Phaeton persisted. "My father, you promised. I am not afraid for my life. Surely your son should be able to guide the car of day."

Finally Apollo yielded with a sigh. He ordered the radiant Hours to harness the horses; he set the sun crown upon the head of Phaeton, and flung wide the palace door.

Before them stretched the wide tracts of sky in which the glorious stars were already paling. Phaeton gathered up the reins and took the whip in his hand.

"One last word, Phaeton, since go you will. Do not use the whip. The horses speed of themselves. Only hold fast the reins and follow the wheel tracks. Do not go too high, or you will burn the heavenly palaces. Do not go too low, or the earth herself may take fire. Keep a middle course. That is safest and best. Farewell!"

Aurora.

The horses sprang forward. With a shout of triumph, Phaeton began his ride.

The horses soon found, however, that they had an unskillful driver. They left the road and galloped more and more wildly. The chariot rocked and bounded from side to side. Phaeton now could scarcely cling to the reins. To look down upon the far-away earth made him so dizzy that he feared to fall.

But worse was to come. The horses had gone so far from their usual track that the sky was now aflame. The clouds were smoking, and soon the great earth herself caught fire.

Harvests withered; cities perished; thousands of people were burned to ashes. Surely there had come a sad and terrible day!

"O Father Jupiter," cried Mother Earth, "come quickly to our aid!"

Father Neptune, god of the sea, raised his head from the seething billows and cried, "O Father Jupiter, come quickly to our aid!"

Jupiter mounted his lofty tower and gazed on the wide scene of disaster. "There is but

one thing to do," he said; and he raised his
terrible right arm.

From it he cast a thunderbolt straight at
the foolhardy Phaeton. The lad fell like a
shooting star down to earth. He lost his life,
but the world was saved.   — Fanny E. Coe.

THE DUCK AND THE KANGAROO

Kan ga roo'   ob jec'tion   re flec'tion

Said the Duck to the Kangaroo,
  "Good gracious! how you hop
Over the fields and the water too,
  As if you would never stop!
My life is a bore in this nasty pond;
And I long to go out in the world beyond:
  I wish I could hop like you,"
  Said the Duck to the Kangaroo.

" Please give me a ride on your back,"
  Said the Duck to the Kangaroo:
" I would sit quite still, and say nothing but
    ' Quack '
  The whole of the long day through;

And we'd go to the Dee, and the Jelly Bo Lee,
Over the land and over the sea :
  Please take me a ride !   Oh, do ! "
  Said the Duck to the Kangaroo.

Said the Kangaroo to the Duck,
  " This requires some little reflection.
Perhaps, on the whole, it might bring me
    luck :
  And there seems but one objection ;

Which is, if you'll let me speak so bold,
Your feet are unpleasantly wet and cold,
  And would probably give me the roo-
  Matiz," said the Kangaroo.

Said the Duck, " As I sate on the rocks,
  I have thought over that completely;
And I bought four pairs of worsted socks,
  Which fit my webfeet neatly;
And, to keep out the cold, I've bought a cloak;
And every day a cigar I'll smoke;
  All to follow my own dear true
  Love of a Kangaroo."

Said the Kangaroo, " I'm ready
  All in the moonlight pale;
And to balance me well, dear Duck, sit steady,
  And quite at the end of my tail."
So away they went with a hop and a bound;
And they hopped the whole world three times
    round.
  And who so happy, oh! who,
  As the Duck and the Kangaroo?
                —EDWARD LEAR.

THE STORY OF GOLGORONDO

buf'fa lo	rhyme	con trived'
doubt'ful ly	cup'board	crev'ice
Mal'le ville	pro vi'ded	droll'er y
Gol go ron'do	or'na ment ed	Phon'ny

[Malleville is a little girl from New York who is spending the winter with her aunt, Mrs. Henry. Beechnut is a boy about fourteen who is hired to do work at Mrs. Henry's. Beechnut tells stories well.]

One bright winter day Malleville came into the shed to watch Beechnut chop wood. Beechnut was glad to have her company. He threw a buffalo robe over some smooth logs at one end of the wood pile. This made a comfortable seat for Malleville.

"I wish you would tell me a story, Beechnut," said Malleville. So Beechnut began as follows : —

"Once there was a giant," said Beechnut, "a great ugly giant, with a terrible face and a large black club. He lived in a den."

"But I don't want to hear such a story

as that," said Malleville. "I don't like to hear about giants, it frightens me so much."

"Oh, this story won't frighten you. This was a good giant."

"But you said he was ugly," replied Malleville.

"He *looked* ugly," said Beechnut, "that was all. I said he looked ugly."

"What was his name?"

"His name," said Beechnut, "his name — why, his name was — Golgorondo."

"I don't believe he was good," said Malleville, shaking her head doubtfully.

"He was, truly," said Beechnut, turning round and looking at Malleville very earnestly. "He was a very good giant, indeed."

"Then what did he want of the great black club?" said Malleville.

"Why, it only looked like a club. It was hollow, and there was something inside. He could unscrew the handle, and draw it out like a sword out of a sword cane."

"What was it inside?"

"It was a long and beautiful feather."

"One day old Golgorondo was sitting at the mouth of his den, sick of a fever, and very thirsty. A boy came along with a red cap on his head.

"'Red Cap, Red Cap,' said Golgorondo, 'I'm feverish and thirsty; I wish you would take this mug and go down to the spring and bring me a mug of cool water.'

"'I can't go now very well,' said Red Cap. 'I want to go and play.'

" ' Very well, run along,' said Golgorondo.

" Presently a girl came by with a green ribbon on her bonnet.

" ' Green Ribbon, Green Ribbon,' said Golgorondo, ' I'm feverish and thirsty ; take this mug down to the spring and get me a drink of good cool water.'

" ' I'm afraid of you,' said Green Ribbon, ' you look so ugly. I'm going to run away.'

" ' Well, run along,' said Golgorondo.

" Pretty soon after that another boy came by, with a blue cap on his head.

" ' Blue Cap, Blue Cap,' said Golgorondo, ' I'm feverish and thirsty ; take this mug and go down to the spring and bring me a drink of good cool water.'

" ' Yes,' said Blue Cap, ' I will.'

" So Blue Cap took the mug and went down to the spring and brought the giant back a mugful of water. When he had drunk it all, Blue Cap asked him if he wanted any more.

" ' One mugful more,' said Golgorondo.

"So Blue Cap went down and brought up one mugful more. Then Golgorondo said, 'Now I shall get well to-night; come and see me to-morrow, and I will reward you for going to the spring and bringing me the mugs of water.'"

"And did he get well?" asked Malleville.

"Yes, and the next day Blue Cap came again."

"And what did the giant give him?"

"A magic bowl," said Beechnut, "a magic silver bowl. He went into his den and unlocked an iron door built into the rocks in the side of his den. It opened into a sort of cupboard, or closet, which was full of treasures. He took out a beautiful silver bowl. It had a sort of saucer under it, and a cover upon the top, and it was ornamented on all sides with beautiful figures, cut in the silver. The knob of the cover, which was used as a handle for taking the cover off, was the figure of a beautiful dog. A little below, upon the side of the cover, was the figure of a hunter and a hare.

"The giant told Blue Cap that the charm of the bowl was in the hunter and the hare. By means of the bowl he could have anything he wanted that was good to eat, provided that he was a good poet.

"The way was to shut up the bowl and take it in his lap, and then say something about the hunter and the hare for one line, and make up another to rhyme with it, asking for whatever he wanted.

"For example, he might say: —

> "'Silver hunter hunting the hare,
> Open your goblet and give me a pear.'

"And then, on opening the bowl, he would find the pear within."

"And would he truly?" asked Malleville.

"Yes," said Beechnut. "Blue Cap took the bowl, put it in his lap and said: —

> "'Silver hunter, silver hare,
> Give me, if you please, a pear.'

"Blue Cap opened the bowl, and there he found inside a large, ripe, mellow, and juicy pear. All this time the giant was sitting by the side of his den."

"I should like such a bowl," said Malleville.

"Blue Cap ate his pear, and then he wanted another; so he put on the cover of the bowl and said again: —

> "'Silver hunter, silver hare,
> I want a sweet and juicy pear.'

"Then he opened the bowl, but there was nothing in it.

"'That won't do,' said Golgorondo. 'The same poetry will not answer twice the same day; you must make some new lines.'

"So Blue Cap thought a minute, and then he said: —

> "'Silver hunter, silver hare,
> Bring me an apple and a pear.'"

"And did he get an apple and a pear?" asked Malleville.

"Yes," said Beechnut; "only the pear was

not quite so large as the other one. Blue
Cap put the apple and the pear in his pocket,
and thanked the giant for his bowl. He
then went away, carrying the bowl under his
arm.

"When he got home, he showed his bowl
to his sister, and they tried to make some new
lines, but they found it very hard. At last
they thought of this : —

> "'Silver hunter, climbing high,
> Give me a piece of apple pie.'"

"And did they get a piece of apple pie?"
asked Malleville.

"A whole one," said Beechnut. "There
was a whole pie, as large as would go into the
bowl, with beautiful figures of dogs, horses,
and huntsmen on the crust."

"Oh, what a good bowl," said Malleville.
"I wish I had such a bowl. The first thing
I would ask for would be for a good large
apple to roast."

"Why, I've got magic enough to get you
an apple to roast," said Beechnut.

So he came to the wood pile where Malleville was sitting and kneeled down.

"I'll get you an apple," said he, "from
under this log."

So he covered over the end of the log with
the bearskin very carefully, and then directed
Malleville to put her two fingers together
upon her knee and to watch them carefully,
while he spoke the magic words.

So Malleville watched her fingers very
closely, while Beechnut repeated these lines
in a measured way, half singing and half
speaking : —

> "Under the end of the beechnut tree,
> Malleville, Malleville, peep and see,
> One for you and none for me,
> Bobolink, bobolink, pee-dee-dee."

Then he lifted up the bearskin a little and
let Malleville peep in. There she saw a fine
large russet apple lying on the chips.

Beechnut had had this apple in his pocket.
While Malleville was watching the ends of
her fingers, he had contrived to reach his arm

back into the wood pile and drop the apple through a crevice. Thence it rolled down to the place under the end of the log where Malleville found it.

Beechnut told Malleville that she must not eat the apple, but must keep it to roast when she went into the house.

That night Malleville began to tell her cousin Phonny the story of Golgorondo and the bowl, as they were going upstairs to bed. They stopped at the head of the stairs to finish the story.

Malleville could not remember the poetry very well. She said that the first line was silver huntsman, silver rabbit, but she could not remember the rest.

Phonny said he guessed it was this : —

> "Silver huntsman, silver rabbit,
> Give me an apple and I'll grab it."

The children laughed loud and long at the drollery, and then went to their rooms.

—Jacob Abbott.

HOW M..t of the big white house across the
hed the gate, she saw Julia Esterhazy

si le'sia
Pris cil'la   are you going, Molly?" Julia
re mem'brance   coming over   ab sorbed'
ex changed'   ir reg'u lar   Es'ter ha zy
Fletch'er

[Mollie and Priscilla were two little cousins. They had
been spending a week together at their grandmother's.

When Mollie was going home, the two little girls exchanged
dimes. Each wished to have a remembrance of the other.]

Molly meant to keep Priscilla's ten cents
always, but she had not been at home many
days before she received a letter from her
cousin that changed her plans. Molly's
mamma read it aloud.

"Dear Molly, — I miss you very, very
much. I cried the day you went, for it was
so lonely. I have spent your ten cents. I
meant to get pink and blue and yellow tissue
paper, but the Fourth of July came and I got
firecrackers instead. They are all gone now,

back into the wood pile and drop ney made through a crevice. Thence it rolle'.

the place under the end of the ıber me by Malleville found it.   ↓nt your ten cents, I want ↓ld Malleville ınine, and then we shall be even. My birthday is the 8th of July. I wish you were my sister.

" Your loving cousin,
" PRISCILLA DRAYTON."

" It is the 8th of July to-day, Molly dear," said Mrs. Benson.

" Then I think I had better go and look around in the shops."

" You will find a great variety of things at Fletcher's," said her mamma; " and if you like, you may go there all by yourself like a grown-up person."

This pleased Molly, and she put on her brown hat and started out with a little shopping bag that her Aunt Ruth had given her at Christmas. Her small purse was in the bottom holding her ten-cent piece. Just as she reached the gate, she saw Julia Esterhazy coming out of the big white house across the way.

".Where are you going, Molly?" Julia asked. "I was coming over to play with you."

"I am going down town shopping," said Molly.

"What are you going to buy?"

"I don't know."

"You don't know what you are going to buy?"

"It may be tissue paper, or it may be paper dolls' furniture, or it may be a new dress for Sylvia or Jane, but whatever it is, it must cost just ten cents." Then Molly told Julia the story of the exchange of the dimes.

"I should get candy if it were mine," said Julia, "and then you could give me some."

"But I don't want to eat up my lovely present," said Molly.

It was a warm day, and the two little girls

were glad to get under shelter away from the hot sun.

Fletcher's was a very delightful shop. It had almost everything in it that any·one could want. In fact, it was so full of charming things that it was hard to make a choice.

Molly's eyes were first fascinated by a card full of paper-doll children, and their pretty blue, red, and white dresses. There was a back and a front view of each little girl, to be cut out and pasted together so as to make a complete person. There were also on the same card a tennis racket and a hoop and a dear little doll in a doll's carriage for the paper-doll children to play with, and a shopping bag and a green watering pot. Molly was afraid that these children and their outfit would cost a great deal of money, ·and that she could not afford to buy them.

"How much are they?" she shyly asked the man behind the counter.

"Twelve cents and a half a card. They

are cheap for that, for they came from
Germany. Do you want one of these
cards ? "

Molly shook her head. "I only have ten
cents," she answered with a sigh.

" I would call it ten cents, seeing that it is
you," he said.

He was a pleasant man, with kind, gray
eyes. "Ten cents is dirt cheap for two children and their entire wardrobe, not to men-
tion playthings," he added.

"Yes, it is very cheap," said Molly.

Julia, meanwhile, had discovered some
paper-doll furniture. One card was full of
kitchen things, and another was devoted to
parlor furniture, while a third displayed a
bedroom set.

"How perfectly beautiful!" Molly said, as
she looked at the little brown bureau with its
white-and-red bureau cover and the red pin-
cushion full of pins.

" What a dear little rug ! " said Julia, point-
ing to a charming brown coonskin rug.

"And look at the towels and the little towel rack," said Molly.

"And the bed and washstand and the pretty blue screen," added Julia.

"See the brown chairs and the dear little brown clock. What fun it would be to cut them out, Julia!"

"Look at the parlor set," said Julia. "See the piano, and the red sofa and chairs, and the tall piano lamp with its red shade."

"The kitchen is a dear place," said Molly. "See the table with a lobster on it in a dish, and the sweet little cooking stove, and the pretty blue dishes in the cupboard; they all look so real."

"See the spice box," said Julia. "Pepper, nutmeg, c-i-n-n-a-m-o-n, cinnamon."

"Oh, look at that dear pussy cat in the kitchen!" said Molly. "How much are these cards?" she asked.

"Ten cents apiece."

"Only ten cents! I don't know which I want the most."

"I should choose the parlor set," said Julia.

"I like the kitchen and the bedroom set the best, because we could have the most fun with them."

"The same things come at five cents a card in a smaller size," the man behind the counter stated.

"At five cents a card! Then I can have two of them, Julia! and I can send one of them to Priscilla, for poor Priscilla has spent all her money on firecrackers, and hasn't anything to remember me by."

"I should keep them both," said Julia. "If she chose to spend her money on firecrackers, that is her lookout. We could have lots more fun with the kitchen and parlor furniture, too."

"Yes, we could," said Molly. "I must look around a little more before I decide," she added prudently. "Oh, Julia, see that pretty pink gingham with white spots on it! How becoming that would be to Sylvia! It takes only a half a yard for her clothes. How much is it for half a yard?"

"It is twenty-five cents a yard," the clerk replied.

"How much would that be for half a yard, Julia?"

"I don't know."

"We don't know how much it would be for half a yard," said Molly, appealingly.

"Well, I'll call it ten cents."

"Ten cents!" said Molly. She was almost sorry, for if it had cost more she could not have bought it, and it would have been a little easier to choose.

"Look at this sweet doll, Molly," said Julia, from the other end of the shop. "A tiny doll and yet so prettily dressed. How much is it?"

"Ten cents."

"Everything is ten cents in this store," said Molly, in despair. "I can't ever decide; but I have so many dolls that I don't really need any more."

" Oh, Molly, see this! " and Julia paused before a tall, round basket. A white card hung above it, and on this card was printed in large black letters : —

CHILDREN'S GRAB BASKET

5 Cents a Grab

EACH ARTICLE FULLY WORTH 7 CENTS

Julia pushed up the cover of the basket, and she and Molly peeped in over the top. There were flat parcels to be seen and three-cornered parcels, and long ones and square ones, and they were all done up in tissue paper. There was something very interesting and mysterious about the grab basket. Those paper packages might have something in them even rarer and more beautiful than the paper-dolls, or the furniture, or the pink gingham.

"You could have two grabs for ten cents," Julia suggested. "You could grab and I could grab, and I could give you my grab."

She was longing to know the contents of a certain interesting irregular parcel.

"The furniture is so sweet," said Molly, "and I am sure I want it."

"The paper-dolls are sweet, too," said Julia.

"Yes, and so is the pink gingham. I shall *have* to grab to decide it."

Meanwhile a more important customer had come in with whom the clerk was absorbed, so Molly went over to him and handed him the ten cents.

"We have decided to have two grabs, and here is the money," she said.

"All right. Did you say you would have

silesia or percaline, madam ?" he asked, turning to the other customer.

"You grab first," said Julia.

Molly looked from the flat parcels to the three-cornered ones and could not decide which to choose.

"I think I will shut my eyes," she said, and she put in her hand at random and pulled out a small, flat parcel. She opened it eagerly, and took out a block of black paper, to be used as a slate, and a pencil with which to write on it. She was sadly disappointed, and felt very much like crying.

"It is a horrid thing," said Julia. "We don't want a paper slate when you have got that nice blackboard. You were very silly to shut your eyes. I shall choose with my eyes open. I am going to take that queer thing that looks as if it might be a doll."

She took out the enticing-looking package and began to untie the string, and presently drew forth a pink-and-white-and-green china vase of a hideous shape. It was too large for dolls, and too small for people, and too ugly to please either.

"That grab bag is perfectly horrid," said Julia.

Molly was sure that she had never been so unhappy. She knew now that it was too late, that she wanted the paper-doll furniture more than anything in the whole world. The two little girls were very sober all the way home. When they reached Molly's gate Julia handed over the vase.

"Take the old thing," she said. "You have got something to remember Priscilla by always now, and you can send the paper slate to her."

"Well, what did you buy, dear?" her mamma asked cheerfully, as Molly came into the parlor.

The little girl found it hard to keep back her tears. Her Aunt Mary and her brother Turner were sitting there too. She felt that it would have been easier to confess her folly to her mother alone.

She held up the vase and the paper block silently.

"The block was a sensible choice," said her mamma, "but I don't see why you chose the vase."

"I didn't choose either of them," Molly burst out. "We grabbed and we got them."

"In short, they chose you," said Turner.

Then the little girl told the whole sad story. "I *did* want the paper-doll furniture so much," she ended.

"Why didn't you buy it, then?" asked her aunt.

"Because we thought it would be more fun to grab."

"This will be a very good lesson for you, Molly," said her aunt. "It is never well to spend money unless you are sure what you are spending it for. I am sorry for you, but you will never be so foolish again."

"There will be time to go to Fletcher's before tea," said Turner. "I will go with you, and we will pretend that the dime I have was Priscilla's and you shall choose what you want all over again."

Molly danced up and down with pleasure, and she and Turner went to Fletcher's together. This time she made her choice very quickly, for she knew just what she wanted. She bought the bedroom set and the kitchen furniture. She remembered Julia's words: "I should keep them both. If Priscilla chose to spend her money on firecrackers, that is her lookout."

But now she herself had spent her money foolishly. If Turner had thought as Julia did, that nobody who had made an unwise investment ought to have anything given her, she would never have had the dear paper-doll furniture. So she kept the kitchen set and sent the bedroom set to Priscilla.

— Eliza Orne White.

THE PARABLE OF THE PRODIGAL SON

And he said, A certain man had two sons:

And the younger of them said to his father, Father, give me the portion of goods that falleth to me. And he divided unto them his living.

And not many days after, the younger son gathered all together, and took his journey into a far country, and there wasted his substance with riotous living.

And when he had spent all, there arose a mighty famine in that land; and he began to be in want.

And he went and joined himself to a citizen of that country; and he sent him into his fields to feed swine.

And he would fain have filled his belly with the husks that the swine did eat: and no man gave unto him.

And when he came to himself, he said, How many hired servants of my father's have bread enough and to spare, and I perish with hunger!

(274)   The Prodigal Son.

I will arise and go to my father, and will say unto him, Father, I have sinned against heaven, and before thee,

And am no more worthy to be called thy son: make me as one of thy hired servants.

And he arose, and came to his father. But when he was yet a great way off, his father saw him, and had compassion, and ran, and fell on his neck, and kissed him.

And the son said unto him, Father, I have sinned against heaven, and in thy sight, and am no more worthy to be called thy son.

But the father said to his servants, Bring forth the best robe, and put it on him; and put a ring on his hand, and shoes on his feet.

And bring hither the fatted calf, and kill it; and let us eat, and be merry:

For this my son was dead, and is alive again; he was lost, and is found. And they began to be merry.

—THE BIBLE.

A CHILD'S THOUGHT OF GOD

They say that God lives very high!
But if you look above the pines,
You cannot see our God.   And why?

And if you dig down in the mines,
You never see Him in the gold,
Though from Him all that's glory shines.

God is so good, He wears a fold
Of heaven and earth across His face —
Like secrets kept for love untold.

But still I feel that His embrace
Slides down by thrills, through all things
    made,
Through sight and sound of every place:

As if my tender mother laid
On my shut lids her kisses' pressure,
Half waking me at night; and said,
" Who kissed you through the dark, dear
    guesser ?"

           —ELIZABETH BARRETT BROWNING.

WORD LIST

Aar'on
ac cord'ing
ac'cu rate ly
ad mi ra'tion
ad vance'
ad ven'tures
Ag a mem'non
a gree'a bly
alm'onds
a maze'ment
am'e thyst
an'cient
and'i ron
a nigh'
an'i ma ted
a noint'ed
anx'ious
A pol'lo
ap peared'
ap'pe tite
as sayed'
At a lan'ta
at tempt'ing
Au gus'ta

au thor'i ties
a void'ing
a wak'ened
a wry'

ban'ter
Be'er she'ba
ben'e fit
Beth'le hem
be ware'
Birk'en head
Bru'in
buf'fa lo

Cam'e lot
carle
Ca'sa bi an'ca
cas'ket
cat'a ract
cau'tion
cau'tious ly
Ce'res
cham'pi on
char'i ot

charm'ing ly
Chaun'cey
Chi ca'go
chim'ney
Chris'tian
chuc'kling
Cin cin na'ti
cit'i zen
clam'ber
clucked
clus'tered
clus'ter ing
coiled
Co logne'
colo'nel
col'um bine
Co lumb'kill
com'fort a ble
com'fort er
com'ic al
com mand'er
com mit'tee
com pas'sion
com plained'

com'pre hend'ed

com'rade

Co'myn

con cern'ing

con di'tion

con geals'

con trived'

Cor'a lie

coun'ter pane'

coun'ter part'

crea'tures

crev'ice

crick'ets

crock

crook'ed

crouched

Crum'pies

cuck'oo pint'

cup'board

cu'ri ous

curt'sied

dam'sel

de cid'ed

del'i cate

de li'cious

de part'ed

dif'fi cul ty

dig'ni fied

di rec'tion

dis'ap peared'

dis as'ter

dis cov'er y

dis cuss'

dis dained'

dis heart'ened

dis or'der

dis sat'is fied

dis tinct'ly

doff'ing

doubt'ful ly

Doug'las

dread'ful ly

droll'er y

duf'fle

ear'nest ly

eat'a bles

Eau Claire'

ek'ron

E'li

E li'za

E liz'a beth

en chant'ed

en cour'aged

en'er gies

e'pha

eph'od

es pe'cial ly

es tab'lished

ex act'ly

ex act'ness

ex am'i na'tion

Ex cal'i bur

ex claimed'

ex er'tions

ex haust'ed

ex'pe di'tion

ex pe'ri ence

ex plo'sion

ex pres'sion

fac'to ry

fam'ine

fa'vor ite

feat

fla min'goes

fore go'

Franz

fright'ened

Fritz

fu'el

fu'gi tive

fur'ni ture

gal'lant

gal lant'

Gal'lo way

Ges'sler

gird'ed

goal

god'dess

Gol go ron'do

Go li'ath

Greece

grieved

griz'zlies

groped

grum'bling

Guin'e vere

gui tar'

haugh'ti ly

hav'er sack

ha'zel

hes'i ta ted

Hip pom'e nes

hon'ey suc kle

hov'el

Hy'a cinth

Hy a cin'thus

ig'no rance

im me'di ate ly

im per'ti nence

im por'tant

im prove'ment

in cau'tious

in'ci dent

in'dia rub'ber

in iq'ui ty

in'ter est ed

in ter rupt'ed

Is'ra el

Jacques

jeal'ous

Je ru'sa lem

Jes'se

ju'ni per

kan ga roo'

ker'chief

knot'ting

la bur'num

lead'en

Le'o de grance

liege

Lith'gow

loft'i ly

lyre

mag nif'i cent

ma hog'a ny

Malle'ville

mar'tyrs

mar'vel ous

mat'tress es

mea'ger

mel'o dy

mem'o ry

Mer'cu ry

mid'ship'man

min'is ter

mis tak'ing

mon'sters

Mont gom'er y

mon'u ment

mor'sel

mor'tals

mu si'cian

neigh'bors

neighed

Nep'tune

nurs'er y

nymphs

o be'di ence

ob'ject

ob jec'tion

ob served'

op'e ra glass

op'por tu'ni ty
or'a cle
or'chard
O'ri ent
or na men'tal
out stretched'
out wit'ted

Pal'es tine
pan'ic-strick'en
par tic'u lar
pas'sa ges
pas'sen gers
pas'sion
pe cul'iar
Pel'li more
pen'guins
per ceived'
per'il ous
per sist'ed
Pe'ter kins
pet'ti coat
pha'e ton
Phil'a del'phi a
Phon'ny
pi az'za
pin'a fore'
plunged

Plu'to
pome'gran'ate
por'rin ger
port cul'lis
por'tion
punch
prai'ries
prec'i pice
prefer'
pre scribe'
pres'ent ly
pres'sure
pre vail'
pris'on er
pro ceed'ed
prod'i gy
prop'er ly
proph'et
Pro ser'pi ne
pro vid'ed
psalm
pto'maine

quan'ti ty
quar'rel ing
quench
quiv'er
quoits

re ceipt'ed
re ceived'
rec on noi'ter ing
re cruit'
re flec'tion
ref'uge
re fused'
re leased'
re peat'ed
re quest'
re solved'
re spond'ed
re store'
re strained'
re tired'
re vealed'
re venged'
rhyme
right'eous ness
ri'ot ous
Ro'man
ruf'fling
run'ci ble
rus'tic
rus'tle

sac'ri fice
sal'lies
Sam'u el

sap′phires	spec ta′tors	un com′fort a ble
Sar′a cens	squash′es	u′ni forms
Sar′a to′ga	squeez′ing	un ti′di ness
sat′is fac′tion	squir′rel	up lift′ed
sat′is fied	star′tling	
scab′bard	stanch	va′cant
scep′tre	sti′fling	veg′e ta bles
screeched	sud′den ly	ven′tured
sem′i cir′cle	Su pe′ri or	ven′ture some
sen′si tive	sur mount′ed	Ve′nus
sep′a rate	sur round′ed	vet′er an
shek′els	Swit′zer land	vi′o lent
shel′ter		vi′sion
shrieked	taxed	
sig′nal	thought′ful ly	war′riors
six′pence	threat′ened	weap′on
Sliev′e league	tour′ney	whirled
slip′per y	tre men′dous	Whit′ta ker
so lem′ni ty	tri′umph	wrath
sol′i tudes	tu′mult	
Sol′o mon	Turk	yon′der
So phi′a	Twom′ly	
Span′iards	ty′rant	Zeph′y rus

SUGGESTIONS IN REGARD TO VOCAL DRILL

To secure good tones from the pupils, plenty of fresh air must be supplied to the lungs. On that account it is desirable, either to have the reading the first lesson in the afternoon programme or to have it follow the gymnastics. During the latter exercise the windows are open and the schoolroom is filled with fresh air.

At the close of the physical exercises, while the pupils are standing, let them give the long vowels preceded by *m* and *l*, after the teacher has herself illustrated the sound. There should be not only class work, but work with individuals. At all times the concert tones should be light and agreeable in quality.

To secure definite suggestions, let us see what the selection "Seven Times One" by Jean Ingelow would demand.

The pitfalls in articulation and pronunciation in this piece are four: (1) the long *u* as in *dew*, *your*, and *you* are; (2) the *ing*; (3) the *o* as in *fellow* and *yellow*; (4) the final *d* in *and* and incidentally the final *r* when followed by *and*.

In the preliminary vowel drill, combinations such as *no*, *new*, *lo*, and *lu* should be especially dwelt upon.

282

The greater part of the time at the teacher's disposal, however, should be devoted to practicing these difficult sounds in combination, for it is as he meets the unforeseen difficulty that the unwary pupil succumbs. It will be observed that the following exercises often kill two birds with one stone.

(1) $\bar{u}$ (danger o͡o) : —

" The *dew* was fall*ing* fast."

" *New* d*u*ties each return*ing* day."

" From morn to noon he fell, from noon to *dewy* eve."

" Like the *dew* on the fountain,
Thou art gone an*d* forever."

" The rose is fairest when 'tis budd*ing new*.
The rose is sweetest washed with morn*ing dew*."

(2) *ing* (also work with *you are* and *your*) : —

You are hid*ing your* face.
You are wav*ing your* arms.
You are build*ing your* nest.
You are ring*ing your* bell.
You are count*ing your* money.
You are shad*ing your* light.
etc.

In certain of the expressions under (2), especially " your face " and " your nest," the teacher may guide the class to the desired inflection that will be needed later when they read, in the poem, " And show me your nest " and " That God has hidden your face."

(3) ō (fellow, yellow) : —

"I kne*w* him, Horatio ; a fell*ow* of infinite jest."

"A primrose by the river's brink.

A yell*ow* primrose was to him

An*d* *it* was noth*ing* more."

(4) and (incidentally final *r*) : —

" Over *and over* again."

" Over the hills *and* fa*r* *a*way."

" Sail*ing* an*d* shin*ing*."

" Roun*d* an*d* low."

" Someth*ing* an*d* everyth*ing*."

In all the work noted above, the pronunciation should be as usual, with no exaggerations of the sounds or combinations in question.

If the interest and pride of the children is enlisted in this preliminary work, the results in the subsequent reading will be potent.

At every step the specific purpose should be clear to the student. The teacher should frequently stop in the midst of the drill to say to the class: "Why are we doing this? What special fault are we trying to correct in this exercise?" If the aim is thus made specific, the pupil's hearty coöperation is insured, and the ultimate results will far exceed what would be the outcome of mere automatic word-calling.

www.ingramcontent.com/pod-product-compliance
Lightning Source LLC
LaVergne TN
LVHW011941060326
832903LV00045B/119